# Critical Thin

# 2 In 1

Why You Should Be Skeptical Of People You Disagree With But Even More Skeptical With People You Agree With

By

Christopher Hayes

# FREE BONUS!

## Free Thinking Cheat Sheet Reveals...

21 timeless thinking principles you need to know to upgrade your thinking and make smarter decisions (not knowing these may hinder you from having the success you'd like to have in life)

## CLICK HERE TO DOWNLOAD FOR FREE!

Or go to www.thinknetic.net or simply scan the code with your camera

# Table of Contents

## Critical Thinking Unleashed

# The Art Of Critical Thinking

# Introduction

The best way to train your mind to think better is through the application of critical thinking. It is a way to improve your quality of thinking through rational and unbiased evaluation of factual evidence. People use critical thinking skills every day, and they are extremely important in several situations, such as the academic and work world.

There are many characteristics of a good critical thinker and plenty of processes and strategies you can use to become a better critical thinker. Certain things completely derail critical thinking and lead to an unproductive, biased, and closed-minded way of thinking that contributes to many of the problems we face in the world today.

If more people used critical thinking skills as often as possible, it could lead to immense innovation, deep conversations, and the elimination of a lot of prejudices.

Critical thinking is difficult to learn. Not everyone is born a natural critical thinker, and to become a critical thinker requires long and consistent practice.

In that case, you might think, why should I even learn critical thinking? What if I'm not a natural-born critical thinker?

Fortunately, there are plenty of ways you can start practicing critical thinking skills, no matter what age you are. If you use them as often as possible before you know it, you will find yourself able to take in large quantities of information, quickly summarize important details, clearly communicate and justify your arguments, and more.

As a researcher who is always on the lookout for ways to improve the lifestyle and thought patterns of myself and others, and has put many of the strategies discussed in this book into practice, I am here to help you learn ways to improve your critical thinking skills.

The journey of critical thinking is vast, and it can be hard to know where to begin. Still, taking it one step at a time and going at your own pace, you will soon find yourself thinking clearer, solving problems in a more organized way, and seeing the world differently.

# The Basics Of Critical Thinking

Critical thinking is something that people use every day, likely without even realizing they are doing it.

There may have been a time where a friend has needed support. Although they did not say it out loud, through interpreting their emotions and body language, you could tell that they needed help, and you offered them advice. Perhaps there was a dispute at work, and you found a way to compromise between opposing ideas. Or maybe you have budgeted your monthly paycheck to determine how much you will have to spend after necessities such as rent and food.

These are all examples of critical thinking. People use it every day to a certain extent, and some use it more than others. However, developing critical thinking skills is essential to starting to live a better quality of life and opening your mind to new possibilities.

According to The Foundation for Critical Thinking, improving the quality of thinking by analyzing, assessing, and reconstructing the particular subject at hand defines critical thinking, and it can be applied. to any subject, content, or problem. [27]

This self-disciplined, self-monitored, and self-corrective thinking involves effective communication. It requires problem-solving abilities and a commitment to overcome our egocentrism and sociocentrism, or preconceived notions about ourselves and the world we are familiar with.

Characterized by careful analysis and judgment, critical thinkers aim their thoughts at the well-founded judgment of a situation based on appropriate evaluation of their surroundings, determining its truth, worth, or value before determining the outcome. [27]

Research into critical thinking shows that typically

human thoughts are predisposed to prejudice, over-generalization, common fallacies, self-deception, rigidity, and narrowness. However, when critical thinking skills are applied, it is a way of training the mind to see past the usual errors in the way people think. It also proves that although people's mind tends to gravitate towards things like narrowness and prejudice without training, the mind can develop good reasoning abilities. [4]

Past research on critical thinking shows there are two intellectual tendencies that people usually fall into: [4]

**The Majority**: One is the tendency of the majority to accept whatever most people believe to be true. In this way of thinking, people look at situations uncritically and feel that because things have been a certain way for some time and because most people feel that way, then it must be true. They do not take it upon themselves to come up with something different.

**The Minority**: Another tendency is to question what is commonly accepted and to seek out answers for oneself. People who fall into this category actively utilize their critical thinking skills in their day-to-day life. They have established more reflective criteria for determining their standards of judgment. Also, they do not take something as being true at face value, and the people around them believe it.

As you embark on your journey to becoming a better thinker, you will no doubt pass through the phases of critical thinking. There are six stages of development you can expect to pass through as you practice and cultivate your critical thinking skills over time. [32]

**The Unreflective Thinker**: Assuming that you are starting at the very beginning when improving your critical thinking skills, the first stage you will go through is the unreflective thinker. Those in phase one are mainly unaware of the important role that critical thinking plays in their lives and cannot also assess their thought patterns and improve them. Although the Unreflective Thinker can have developed a variety of skills up to this point, they are unaware that they possess them.

**The Challenged Thinker**: It is this phase where you realize the important role that critical thinking plays in your life. They realize that high-quality thinking comes through reflective thinking, and they recognize that most thinking is flawed. Although they have limited critical thinking skills, they might feel that the skills they have unconsciously developed make them better thinkers than they are, and they have to accept the challenge to improve.

**The Beginning Thinker**: In the third phase, you have accepted the challenge to become a better thinker and are already taking steps to improve. At this stage, people realize the basic problem in their thinking and are taking steps to correct them. At this phase, you also realize the key concepts of critical thinking, such as concepts, assumptions, inferences, implications, and points of view. Additionally, beginner thinkers can appreciate criticism of their current thought processes because it allows them to see how they can improve.

**The Practicing Thinker**: At this phase, people have a sense of the habits they need to develop to become full-fledged critical thinkers. They also understand the need to fix their thinking systematically and can actively analyze their thinking in different domains. At this phase, you will have enough skills to monitor your thoughts regularly and correct them on the spot. You can also recognize your egocentricity, the role they play in your critical thinking, and how to correct them.

**The Advanced Thinker**: At this point, the good habits of thought you have established are starting to pay off. You are actively analyzing your thinking in all of the specific domains of your life and have insight into problems on a deeper level. Advanced thinkers are very knowledgeable of what it takes to assess their thinking for clarity and precision regularly. So, they are always on the road to improvement.

**The Accomplished Thinker**: Being at the final stage does not mean you would have mastered critical thinking completely because critical thinking is always an ongoing learning process. However, at this stage, you will have deeply internalized the basic skills of thought, so your critical thinking is conscious and highly intuitive.

In addition to improving your quality of thinking, critical thinking serves to help you organize your thoughts. Instead of letting emotions get in the way of your thinking, it allows you to take a step back, regroup, and approach your thoughts from a more objective standpoint. This self-guided and self-disciplined type of thinking attempts to help you to reason at the highest level of quality in a fair-minded way.

Utilizing critical thinking skills makes a positive impact on your quality of life as people who think critically tend to live rationally, reasonably, and empathically. This is because they do not let emotions and subjectivity get in the way of seeing things for what they truly are. They know of the flawed nature of human thinking when it is left unchecked and strive not to let their ego or their social environment get in the way. [4]

Further, critical thinking involves thinking outside of the box. However, if you want to think outside of the box, you need to establish creativity within your mind. [20]

Critical thinking and creativity go hand in hand. While critical thinking involves thinking clearly and rationally, following the rules of logic and scientific reasoning, creativity involves coming up with new and useful ideas as well as alternative possibilities. Creativity is necessary to solve problems; however, critical thinking is essential when it comes to evaluating and improving these ideas. Both are necessary, and both are needed for people to prosper ultimately. [20]

Although creativity tends to be a little more spontaneous than critical thinking, it is similar to critical thinking in how it follows a step-by-step process. You have likely done something similar to this before without even realizing it. The Creativity Cycle involves four steps [20]:

**Preparation**: This step is just like it sounds; you are setting up the framework for whatever it is you are trying to come up with. That means gathering information. You can read up on it in the library or online. You can also talk to other people to find out more. At this stage, you are collecting everything that might be relevant to the situation without very much filtering or analysis, which comes in the next step.

Imagine an artist who is putting together their next big work of art with the theme of the environment. They certainly can pull out their canvas and just make things up as they go along, but they want this creative masterpiece to be a thoughtful one. So, they pull together as many resources as they can find to make this as in-depth of a piece as they can make it.

**Exploration**: At this stage, you have collected all the information you need. Now it is time to look at what you have. This can include classifying your material, organizing it, and looking at it from different perspectives. While devoting your attention to what you have found, you might find some things might not be as useful to you as you thought, or you might find gaps that you need to fill.

Think of the artist who, at this stage, will have

gathered everything they can have to do with the environment, such as physical materials as well as written research. At this phase, the creative person will inspect everything to determine what they can and cannot use for their project as well as starting to piece together what the final project will be like.

**Incubation**: Sometimes, it is difficult to come up with a final plan, and, at that point, it's a good idea to pause and let the idea sit with you for a while. Set the task aside for a moment, relax, and come to it later. Chances are an idea will come to you when you are listening to music or taking a walk. The incubation stage lets you come back to the project later with a fresh eye and new ideas.

**Verification**: Once you've come back to your project, it is time to see if it can work. This means putting everything together and seeing what the outcome will be. If the project was unsuccessful and didn't turn out the outcome you wanted, then it's time to go back to the drawing board. If it was successful, then look back on what went well so you can repeat the process.

The Creativity Cycle is a lot more common than you might think. How many items, projects, or programs can you think of that may have followed this same process? Maybe at their verification phase, they found that their project wasn't as viable as they thought and had to start from the beginning, or maybe it ended up being very successful and well known on the first try.

Although creativity is a little different from critical thinking, the two are like a brother and sister. True creativity uses critical thinking skills, and creativity enhances critical thinking. While you will find the steps in The Creativity Cycle differ from the steps in critical thinking, you will also find they have some similarities. [20]

## The Opposite To Critical Thinking

Critical thinking is an active way of thinking where a person develops a set of skills to conceptualize, apply, analyze, and evaluate the information given to them. Methods such as observation, experience, reflection, or communication help to develop critical thinking skills. These methods develop one's beliefs and actions to organize thoughts to form opinions from an objective standpoint and are essential to creative thought.

Those who are not using their critical thinking skills fall into the habit of passive thinking.

Passive thinkers operate under the mindset that things are happening to them instead of making things happen themselves, and they are not responsible for the things that happen to them. Instead, they fall into the "pack" mentality, meaning they go along with what others think instead of using the analytical skills of a critical thinker to discover answers for themselves. [25]

If someone says something is true, the passive thinker might simply believe it is so. If the people around them have a certain mindset, the passive thinker will not take it upon themselves to find a different perspective.

The quality of life of someone who continuously uses passive thinking reflects their mindset. Eventually, they will end up believing that nothing is their responsibility. Additionally, they go through life, making passive associations. They allow whatever thoughts float through their mind to be at the forefront of their beliefs. Instead of the clarity and awareness that comes with critical thinking, they live blurrily. This means that their thoughts and beliefs change easily. [25]

Part of passive thinking is gut thinking. This involves making decisions based on instinct instead of putting thought into what you are doing. It involves intuitive thinking, which is a feeling or sense that does not use rational processes to come to any conclusion. Think of it as having your brain on autopilot, and you are just casually going along with it. [18]

There are cases when gut thinking comes in handy. Have you ever been in a situation where something just does not seem right? An everyday example might include getting such a great deal on something you are trying to buy, that it seems too good to be true. You can't exactly pinpoint why, but intuition will tell you that it does not seem like a good idea. Sure enough, you turn it down and find out later that it was a scam.

We develop good intuition through practice. It comes from years of experience that allows you to discover just how the world and the people in it work. However, you should not rely on intuition for every decision you make. [25]

In situations that require a major decision, whether in your personal life, at work, or any situation that affects others, it is often best to weigh the pros and cons of that decision, think it through, and analyze it carefully before coming to any conclusion on it.

I can consider passive thinking a cause of many of the world's problems, such as racism, xenophobia, and religious extremism. All of those ideologies have one thing in common: they result from closed-mindedness and an absence of true critical thinking as they fall into the trap of passive thinking.

A racist person is more likely the result of their environment. Someone with this mindset may have spent much of their time surrounded by people open about their racist ideologies. Because they have used no critical thinking skills into the matter, they do not question the wrongful way of thinking it pushed onto them. Other people believe it, so it must be correct.

They do not take the initiative to discover for themselves other perspectives; instead, they remain set in the way of other people's mindset, not bothering to find their own.

If they were to use critical thinking skills into the matter, they would question the validity of the situation. They would take the initiative to do their research on other ethnicities and cultures to understand them. They would find articles and news stories of ideologies opposite of their own to learn how others think. They might also go out and find people different from them to get to know them.

After putting into practice a set of critical thinking actions, they can form their own opinion of other races instead of following the majority they had been surrounded by.

On a day-to-day basis, the lack of critical thinking can make everyday interactions much less meaningful than they could be. There are a few reasons society could be at fault for this. [4]

One reason focuses on the historical roots of individuals. From an early age, we teach people that having unconventional ideas is wrong. We learned that it is wrong to question the status quo or to have different views than others. It conditions them on what is right, what is wrong, what is normal, and what is abnormal; and the moment they think about falling out of line with those preconceived set of standards, they feel that they are doing something wrong. [4]

Another could be the consumption of popular culture. With the omniscience of the internet, it is easy for people, especially young people, to be conditioned by what they see. Whether it is television or social media, the constant barrage of things can make their imagination insular. They take what they see as a standard of how they should think and act and do not question it.

## Critical, Passive, And Gut Thinking

Overall, critical thinking leads us to unlock our intellectual independence. It helps to move us away from rushed conclusions, mystification, and reluctance to question received wisdom, tradition, and authority. Unlike passive thinking, it moves us towards intellectual discipline, a clear expression of ideas, and acceptance of personal responsibility for our thinking.

According to the Foundation of Critical Thinking, critical thinkers can [6]:

- Raise vital questions when it comes to solving problems by forming their questions clearly and precisely.
- Gather and assess information related to a particular topic by using abstract ideas to interpret the topic more effectively.

- Come to well-reasoned conclusions as well as test them among relevant criteria and standards.
- Be open-minded when it comes to alternative systems of thought because they can recognize and assess their assumptions, implications, and practical consequences.
- Communicate effectively with others by figuring out solutions to complex problems.

In many cases, non-intuitive thinking, or critical thinking, is the best way to make decisions over intuitive thinking.

This is especially true when there is no obvious solution to a problem. The passive or intuitive thinker might go with the first answer that pops into their mind, but it might not end up being the correct answer.

Instead of just going with the first thing that enters

your mind or going along with whatever someone else told you, critical thinking allows you to ask certain questions before you make a definitive conclusion: [25]

- Does this make sense?
- Why does it make sense? Or why not?
- How can I apply it?

Unlike passive thinking, critical thinking allows you to keep an open mind to new information as well as test new experiences and information against past experiences and information. Upon testing the information given to you, you will have a well-rounded frame of reference to either keep the opinion you held at first or form a new opinion.

During passive thinking, your mind is just going through the motions accepting what comes your way putting no intellectual thought forward to challenge it. There are several ways to grasp critical thinking ideas that not only provide insight during the present moment but enrich your life and strengthen your cognitive processes. [6]

**Gaining Experience**: Experience is the world's best teacher. By gaining experience in as many areas as possible, you expand your knowledge base on a variety of topics and are better able to make connections when most needed. Experience teaches you what problems or objectives are straightforward and what is not, what to look for in several situations, and what issues are the most important for you to address.

This can apply to any life experience, whether it is gaining experience in your field of work, as a new parent, someone just beginning their college education, and more. No matter where you find yourself, the experience will be essential in the long run to thinking critically about the positions you find yourself in.

**Experimentation**: This can help you discover inconsistencies in a situation or train of thought. One way you can do this is by tinkering or doing a series of problem-solving activities that will enable you to learn by trial and error. This is a powerful critical thinking skill born out of curiosity and developed through discovery. In some cases, experimenting can be a leisurely activity, something done just for fun with no goals, deadlines, or pressure but serves to let you learn at your own pace. Other times it can lead to a significant discovery that can be useful to you.

One example of experimentation is working on some mechanical object, like a car. If you have an interest in cars, or even if you don't, and you take the time to poke around seeing how things work, this could yield several results. For one thing, you could learn something you didn't know before, which could be useful to you the next time your car breaks down. Another benefit may be that you become equipped with the information you can use to critically assess a situation such as someone trying to sell you something you don't particularly need for the car or any other situation where you need to decide on the car.

**Learning**: They say learning does not end once school is over. The more you grow your knowledge base, the more you know about all the little nuances and subtleties of life. The more you read, research, learn from others, and partake in any other method to expand your knowledge of various topics, the more of a capacity you will have for critical thinking.

Critical thinking takes practice, and no one will use critical thinking every second of every day. The mind tends to wander, so everyone will tend to irrational or passive thoughts now and then.

However, as a self-directed and self-disciplined mode of thought, critical thinking yields results and benefits when used correctly. This is where creativity comes into play. Thinking critically is the basis for coming up with new and innovative solutions to problems we face every day.

Used in a group, critical thinking can be even more useful not only to individuals but the world. The more people gathered from various and diverse disciplines, assembling to solve our many problems, the better our society will be prepared for the future.

An everyday example involves a school. Several teachers have noticed they have students in their classes who are falling behind in mathematics. One teacher brings it up to their colleague who shares their struggle, and they think about how to fix the problem.

At their next planning meeting among the rest of the teachers in their department, they share their observations, and other teachers express that they have noticed the same thing. Everyone has a shared problem; now, the question remains of what to do about it.

So, they start brainstorming. They collectively come up with ideas that range from individual tutoring to having their students stay after class. After weighing all points, they concluded that an after-school math tutoring program would be the best way to solve the problem. They then work together to arrange how the program will work.

On a larger scale, take, for example, a big county where people in different areas have different needs. The needs of the northern half of the county differ vastly from those of the southern half, and both sides feel like the county government is not hearing their concerns.

The leaders of the county recognize this after complaints from throughout the area and come together to work towards a solution. The main question among them is what is the best way to address every part of the county and come up with objective and implementable solutions.

The group recognizes that town hall meetings have been successful in the past at drawing a substantial group of people. They hold individual meetings in various cities and towns throughout the county to get a hyper-local view of what people need. Also, they compiled written feedback and then brought everyone together to review those plans before implementing the following year.

# Premises And Arguments

Critical thinking is a rational thought pattern. It involves analyzing the problem at hand, thinking it through thoroughly allowing you to avoid rushed conclusions, and planning a well-developed argument before drawing any conclusions. These characteristics are essential for organizing your thoughts to develop good premises and arguments.

At its core, a premise is a proposition that we base an argument on. From an argument, you can then conclude. We can also think of premises as the reasons and evidence behind a conclusion. [9]

In a deductive argument, a premise can be a major or minor proposition of the argument in which we draw two conclusions from, also known as a syllogism, to draw logical conclusions. For example, "All mammals are warm-blooded," would be considered a major premise, "Whales are mammals," is the minor premise. Therefore, the conclusion to this argument would be, "Whales are warm-blooded."

Premises are common in philosophy and writing. In philosophy, arguments are more concerned with a set of premises that support a conclusion more so than disputes among people. [24]

Also, in philosophical arguments, we consider an argument valid if it follows logically through its premises, but the conclusion can still be invalid. The process of concluding then involves a process of deductive reasoning.

You can say that "men are tall," followed by, "the singer Prince is a man," and conclude that "Prince is tall," but this would be an inaccurate conclusion considering that Prince was known for being short at only five feet two inches tall.

In writing, particularly nonfiction writing, premises typically follow the same rules as philosophical premises. The Purdue University Online Writing Lab (OWL) defines premises as an assertion of a conclusion based on logical premises and calls the syllogisms used in philosophy the simplest sequence of logical premises and conclusions. [24]

The difference between premises in philosophy and writing is that nonfiction writing, in general, rarely distinguishes between major and minor premises.

In nonfiction writing, it is common to see premises used as the basis of an editorial or an opinion piece or a letter to the editor. So, for example, your first premise might be, "Nonrenewable resources do not exist in infinite supply," and the second premise would be, "Coal is a nonrenewable resource." So, your conclusion is, "Coal does not exist in infinite supply." Not necessarily a major and minor premise, such as in philosophy, but the same rules still apply.

In fiction writing, the premise serves as the foundation for your story but does not necessarily try to form an argument like philosophical and nonfiction premises do. The characters of the plot then prove or disprove the argument. [24]

If we take the story "The Three Little Pigs," the premise there is that "Foolishness leads to death and wisdom leads to happiness." The argument itself does not prove its point through major and minor premises, but the characters and the plot of the story make the argument and prove it to be true by the end.

We can use premises in a variety of other arguments. Not limited to just philosophy and writing, we can use premises in science, theology, and more.

# Are There Good And Bad Arguments?

Anyone can come up with a premise for an argument. However, that does not necessarily mean your argument is good. This is where your critical thinking skills come into play. It takes a little organization, problem-solving, and analyzing to come up with a good argument that makes sense and effectively supports the case you are trying to make.

The truthfulness or falsity of your argument does not so much have anything to do with ethics or morals as much as it is your reasons for giving the argument accurately. The reasons for the argument must be closely associated with the truth, meaning your premises must be correct to come up with a truthful argument. Good reason makes belief more probable, and vice versa. The very best reasons make it certain. [12]

There are a few characteristics essential to a good or truthful argument. [12]

- **Valid**: If your argument is invalid, it will ultimately lead to a bad argument. The intention would give conclusive support for its conclusion instead of building up to the conclusion through an argument that makes sense.

- **Strong**: A strong argument is difficult to dispute. In a weak argument, many other viable conclusions are possible, which results in your conclusion to fall apart. Strong arguments are the kinds of arguments you want to strive for.

- **Sound**: A sound argument involves true premises. This is essential in planning a good argument. If your premises are not true, your argument falls apart, and your conclusion ends up being false.

- **Cogent**: This means your argument is clear, logical, and convincing. Think of your argument being cogent as the end goal of your argument: if your premises are false and your argument is invalid and weak, then your argument is not cogent and, therefore, a bad argument.

Where good arguments have their reasons based on truth, bad arguments have their reasons based on falsehood. These arguments are misleading, whether or not intentional, and dismantle what could be a valid, strong, sound, and cogent argument.

Like truthful arguments, there are also a few characteristics that go along with false arguments. [13]

**Dubious Premises**: Arguments that depend on dubious premises are inherently false arguments because they are suspicious, untrustworthy, unreliable, and questionable. They depend on the hope that the audience will misunderstand or completely fail to understand the argument. They can also benefit from a particular context such as an advertisement that would say a product is a high quality although it is not.

A dubious premise can mislead by assuming the answer to a question before it even comes up, such as, "Have you stopped cheating?" Additionally, dubious premises may lead to arguments which contain premises that are insufficiently informative or complete nonsense.

**Fallacies**: A fallacy often arises from vagueness, ambiguity, and equivocation in the premise, which makes it impossible for the audience to accept them as true. Fallacies can also occur when the conclusion of the argument either supports the premise or merely restates the premise. These fall apart because they end up not being derived from the argument itself.

Fallacies can be even further weakened by irrelevance, meaning that the argument brings in irrelevant information intending to divert the audience's attention away from the argument itself.

There are a few different types of fallacies that intend to divert attention away from the argument. The most common are ad hominem fallacies directed at the opinion holder in the argument. We can consider these abusive attacks or circumstances. Tu quoque fallacies accuse the opinion holder of inconsistency or hypocrisy. They fail to address the opinion holder's argument itself. Straw man fallacies set up inaccurate reconstructions of someone's argument in an attempt to criticize it. Finally, ad populum fallacies try to convince the audience that the argument is correct because it is popular.

**Hasty Conclusions**: Arguments with hasty conclusions tend to employ what is called enthymematic premises. These premises intentionally suppress, accidentally overlook, and are dubious. These hasty conclusions also employ other types of fallacies and diversions to draw their conclusion faster. Another way that arguments can draw hasty conclusions is by appealing to ignorance to support a conclusion as they suggest that if something is not true, then it must be false.

## How Premises Lead To A Conclusion, And How To Analyze Premises?

Premises are essential to composing a truthful argument. What follows the argument is the conclusion. There are specific ways to get there from the formulation of your premise.

We can consider premises and conclusions the basic building blocks of an argument. We know that premises are assertions or pieces of evidence that lead to a conclusion, but the trouble is how we get to the conclusion in the first place.

First, let's look at the conclusions. We can regard a conclusion as an assertion that your audience will not readily accept. For example, your conclusion can be, "The lake is deep." The person to whom you are presenting this conclusion can easily follow up with,

"Well, what evidence do you have that this lake is deep?" [14]

All conclusions need to have at least one premise that supports it. Think of it as a paper written for a class. They start with a thesis, followed by several paragraphs that contain your main points, and they always end with a conclusion that is supported by the preceding argument.

So, taking the above example, if you change your argument to add the premise that "All lakes in this region are deep," you can conclude that this lake is deep.

Sometimes differentiating between premises and conclusions can be confusing. To make things easier, look for indicator words that signal which part of the argument is the premise and which is the conclusion. Also known as joining words, these act as a transition between the premise and conclusion. [14]

Indicator words for premises include words such as because, but, since, given that, and or considering that. For conclusions, indicator words include "therefore," "thus," "which follows," "that consequently," and so.

These are useful to know if you have an argument where the conclusion comes before the premise. For example, in the argument, "You need to drink water because your body cannot survive without water," you can tell the premise follows the conclusion by the indicator word "because."

There is a process you can follow for analyzing a premise. This is a way of evaluating the information given to us in a disciplined way.

**Analyzing**: This is an important first step because it involves examining the argument methodically and in detail to get to know the structure of the argument. This includes breaking down what parts of the arguments are premises and which parts are conclusions; that way, you can then find out what the purpose of the argument is.

So if we analyze the argument, "Poodles are small dogs, and I have heard that they do not shed, so you should get a poodle," we can determine that "poodles are small dogs," and, "I have heard that they do not shed," are the premises and, "you should get a poodle," is the conclusion.

**Conceptualizing**: This means forming an idea about something. When you conceptualize, it helps to produce an image in your mind or come up with an analogy that you can relate to much easier. In the case of the poodle, you might imagine what a poodle looks like; a small, fluffy dog. You can also imagine the dog in comparison to your home. How small would you want your dog to be? How tall is it compared to your furniture? Can you imagine how easy or difficult it would be to clean up after a dog if it shed a lot?

**Defining**: Defining something involves stating or describing the exact nature, scope, or meaning of something. In the case of your argument, at this step, you would try to explain, interpret, and clarify it. Here, break down each premise and interpret exactly what it means. "Poodles are small dogs." What would you consider to be a small dog? Maybe something between one and two feet tall. "I have heard that they do not shed?" You know that shedding involves a dog losing a lot of hair throughout the day that the owner has to clean up from furniture, carpets, and clothing.

**Examining**: Investigating involves inspecting something thoroughly. Here you want to determine the nature or condition of your argument while even testing the knowledge of it. This is where you ask yourself some additional questions about the premise. Is there any way that you can dispute this? Are there any alternative arguments to it?

**Inferring**: At this step, you ask yourself if there is anything you can deduce or conclude from the premise. Naturally, this might be the conclusion that "you should get a poodle," but ask yourself if there are any alternative conclusions that you can infer from the premise. If not, you can consider this a deductive argument.

**Listening**: This is important in any situation, and here it will be key to ensuring that you have heard every aspect of the argument, so you have everything you need to draw your conclusion from it and determine that it is, in fact, a truthful argument.

**Questioning**: We know that a deductive argument leaves no room for you to question its conclusion. At this step, go over each premise again and see if you can point out questions about the conclusion that might prove it to be false.

**Reasoning**: This is the act of thinking about something logically and sensibly. Does each premise make sense? We know that poodles are considered small dogs, as well as the fact that they don't shed. Based on the circumstances of these premises, does the conclusion that you should get a poodle also seem logical?

**Synthesizing**: This is the stage where you put it all together. You have thoroughly examined each premise and asked all the questions that you can. If there are no further questions or alternatives, it is safe to say that what you have is a truthful argument. The conclusion, "You should get a poodle," meets the criteria of being a valid, sound, strong, cogent, and deductive argument.

## Deductive And Ampliative Arguments

Another sign of a good argument is if it is deductive. One way to determine if an argument is substantial or not is to determine how well the premises of the argument supports its conclusion. The more they support the argument, the more deductive the argument is.

We can describe deductive arguments as arguments to guarantee that the truth of the conclusion as long as the premises of the argument are true. This means the argument is deductively valid. [9]

In these types of arguments, the premises must provide such strong support for the conclusion that if the premises are true, then it would be impossible to determine that the conclusion is false, thus a stronger argument. As long as the premises guarantee, the conclusion is true; this is considered a valid argument. Valid arguments have true premises, thus are considered sound. [9]

To look at an example of a deductive argument: "It is sunny in the city. If it is sunny in the city, Joe will not take an umbrella with him. Therefore, he will not carry an umbrella."

Both the premises of the argument support the conclusion, so it makes sense to conclude that Joe will not take an umbrella with him because it is sunny in the city. The argument is sound, and it is also valid because the premises guarantee that the conclusion is true, and they give no room for evidence that would say otherwise.

The opposite of deductive arguments is inductive, or ampliative reasoning. While deductive arguments find their conclusion based on the premises provided in the argument, ampliative arguments interpret the evidence based on the conclusion. It amplifies the evidence through methods of generalizing, predicting, or uncovering the best account of this evidence. [9]

Ampliative arguments attempt to prove that their argument is strong enough that if this argument were to be true, then it would be unlikely that the conclusion is false. Ampliative arguments are not as definitive as deductive arguments as it bases their strength on the degree to which we consider their argument likely to be true.

To take an example of an ampliative argument: "Today Ashley said she is tired, so Ashley told her mom she is tired."

This conclusion of this ampliative argument is not as definite as it would be if it were a deductive argument. It leaves a lot of room to dispute the conclusion. You could ask why Ashley is tired or does Ashley show any evidence of being tired.

The addition of a premise creates ampliative

arguments that are more deductive arguments. This provides evidence to support the argument. Think of the difference between deductive and ampliative arguments as a threshold: ampliative arguments leave room to add more premises, or evidence, to support their conclusion while deductive arguments do not.

So, if you were to add another premise to this ampliative argument, it becomes stronger.

"Ashley worked a long shift today. Ashley is tired. So, Ashley told her mom she is tired because she worked a long shift."

The ampliative argument becomes more valid with the addition of the premise that justifies the conclusion of Ashley telling her mom she is tired.

A lot of times, people use ampliative arguments as if

they were deductive.

Keep in mind the key differences between deductive and ampliative arguments. It is easy to get them confused because the only thing separating an ampliative argument from a deductive argument is the addition of a premise that makes the argument more specific. [15]

We can think of deductive arguments as arguing from a general idea to a specific one, while ampliative arguments would argue from a specific idea to a general one. The two are related; however, it is only one key phrase that separates them. [15]

Deductive arguments attempt to provide grounds for making their conclusion, and if they succeed, we consider the argument valid. Most importantly, the premises of the argument must be true. If both things are the case, then you can consider it a sound and truthful argument.

Although just as common as deductive arguments, ampliative arguments attempt to provide the grounds for the argument to be likely or probable.

# Main Features Of A Critical Thinker

Most people have to know someone in their life who consistently puts into practice critical thinking skills. This is probably the person who is very knowledgeable about certain topics, forms their own opinion about things, always coming up with solutions to problems, and usually knows the best way of going about solving these problems.

Have you ever thought about what sets them apart as a critical thinker, though? Are there any characteristics they seem to display in everyday situations that distinguish them as someone who uses critical thinking skills daily?

To illustrate the different characteristics of certain people, think of two people faced with a situation. These people would be considered the critical thinker and the passive thinker.

Both people work in a retail store and face a situation where a customer wants to return an item. Returns at this store are tricky, and they are not sure of how to do it on their own. The differences in their thought patterns determine how each person will respond to this situation.

The passive thinker is not one to be creative. Although they received training for the return process, returns are tricky, and they have difficulty remembering all the steps.

They do not take the time to assess the situation and look for the resources at their disposal that will help them perform the return. Instead of examining the situation thoroughly, they don't put forth the effort to find a solution to the problem.

The passive thinker takes up the mentality that they don't know what to do, and devise that a task is impossible. They may feel defeated, or they may even convince themselves that it does not matter. They tell the customer, "Sorry, I don't know how to do that. Come another time," and leave the situation as it is.

However, the critical thinker takes a different approach. Curious and resourceful, the critical thinker immediately takes it upon themselves to find a solution. With an open-minded perspective and the ability to handle uncertainty, they walk through all the steps of critical thinking as they try to find an answer.

They run through all of their options: clicking around in the computer system to figure it out, looking through the instruction manuals that the store provides, calls customer service and the store manager. Finally, after exhausting all of their options and analyzing the situation as thoroughly as possible, they find an answer to the problem.

Certain characteristics distinguish a critical thinker

from a passive thinker. This involves everything from how they view the world, their approach to a problem, and the steps they take to find answers.

The passive thinker gives up easily, has a narrow perspective, and does not take the initiative to discover answers that aren't very clear to them.

However, there are a few different characteristics that set critical thinkers apart from others.

**Curiosity**: You could say this is the first step towards becoming a critical thinker. People who are good critical thinkers have to be curious about the situations they find themselves in and just life. This is how the critical thinker asks the questions that set them off to discover new perspectives and ideas. They ask the who, what, when, where, why, and how questions that allow for fully informed, well-rounded answers, and even innovation.

To take the retail situation, for example, the difference in how the critical thinker and the passive thinker approached the situation began with curiosity. The passive thinker did not bother to ask themselves questions about the situation. On the other hand, the critical thinker asked how I can do this. They wanted to gain a new skill and were curious about how to achieve what had been so difficult for them in the past.

**A Wide Perspective**: This is another characteristic essential to being a critical thinker. If someone is narrow-minded and not open to new possibilities, then they will not find themselves able to accept new ideas, new strategies, and be able to accept new possibilities. A wide perspective enables the critical thinker to step outside their box and find out what lies ahead of them.

In the retail example, the critical thinker could use the resources at their disposal, such as the guidebook the store provided to them and the customer service line because they were open-minded about the possibilities of how to perform this return and help the customer. In contrast, a passive thinker's mind did not get to the idea of using any resources. With the narrow-minded thinking of "I don't know what to do so I can't do this," it is a negative premise, a closed perspective, and did not leave them with the open-mindedness necessary to solve the problem at hand.

**Broad Knowledge**: What you may have noticed about the critical thinkers in your life is that they have a vast knowledge of a variety of topics. Often critical thinkers read books, consuming news about current events, and going out to experience things firsthand, like going to a museum.

Learning is such an essential step to strengthening your critical thinking skills because the more you know about a range of topics, the more often you will think critically about any situation or topic that presents itself to you. If someone is very knowledgeable about the history, they will notice patterns in current events that mirror past events and infer what happened at a previous point in time. Or if someone possesses a lot of knowledge in politics, they have more of an advantage when it comes to the ability to think critically about political events such as presidential debates.

**Being Properly Informed About the Subject**: When it comes to thinking critically, while a lot of knowledge is important, it is even more important to have accurate knowledge. A person can learn as much as they want, but if they are not properly informed about a subject, then their knowledge is useless.

Take the history buff again. A person can be extremely interested in history and have consumed several books about various historical periods. But if their knowledge of a subject is completely misinformed, for example, Ancient Rome, then their argument that present-day America is mirroring the fall of Rome becomes inaccurate.

**Examining the Reasoning and Possible Biases and The Assumptions Behind Them**: Not only can critical thinkers formulate accurate and sound reasoning behind an argument, but they also possess the ability to recognize any kind of bias among that reasoning, whether it is their own or the biases of someone else. If given a political argument, they can recognize the bias that comes with party affiliation and separates that from the situation to create a sound argument. Or if a new teacher comes into their school and they are wonderful, the critical thinker can put aside their own biases and objectively explain why this teacher is so great.

**The Possession of Reasoning Based on Sound Consistent Logic**: If the logic behind the reasoning of an argument is inconsistent, then ultimately, the entire argument falls apart. If the premises of an argument are, "Water is wet, rain is water," but they conclude with, "The rain is not wet," there is no logic behind that argument. Not only does the critical thinker possess this reasoning, but they do it with no emotions or social pressure behind it. Their own emotions or the pressure they experience from their peers only served to make their argument biased, which they try to avoid in the first place.

**Ability to Handle Uncertainty**: This is very important in situations where critical thinking is necessary. Sometimes there is a problem that needs to be solved, and the answers are not obvious. The critical thinker does not fall apart and give up when uncertainty arises. Like the retail worker, the critical thinker possesses the ability to remain calm in uncertain situations. They can determine the steps for the task-at-hand while staying level-headed.

**Aware of Their Own Areas of Ignorance**: Besides being aware of their own biases, the critical thinker is also aware of their ignorance in a situation. Someone can't know everything, so when the critical thinker encounters something they are unsure of, they recognize it and try to find the answers. On top of this, they do not come up with information to fill in what they do not know.

**They Can Wait for Valid Evidence and Evidence-Based Answers**: Evidence is essential to forming a valid and sound argument. You cannot draw a good conclusion from an argument without sound evidence. Critical thinkers recognize how important evidence is to an argument and will find sufficient evidence to support their argument no matter what.

# Things That Sabotage Critical Thinking

Overall, there are too many reasons people do not think critically. One of them is that people have become so busy (or lazy) they allow other people to think for them. Another is that it is so easy to distort the truth through what we call perception.

The critical thinker, however, challenges environmental myths, distortions of the truth, special political interests, Gladwell, corporate bureaucracy, groupthink, and anything that goes against good, old-fashioned investigative thinking and critical thinking. [17]

Certainly, anyone can learn to think more critically if they put their mind to it and commit to practicing it daily. However, most people do not think critically as much as they think they do. One thing that sabotages critical thinking in anyone is that most people try to avoid thinking.

Thinking critically takes a lot of effort, much more effort than most people want to put in on a day-to-day basis. There are a few techniques that people employ, so they don't have to think critically as much as they should. [17]

The first is the "monkey mind," what Buddhists used to describe mental distraction. With this technique, the mind wanders and jumps from thought to thought with no direction. Picture it like a monkey jumping back and forth from tree to tree, trying to let out its frustrations.

Another technique is the "gator brain." This is the primitive part of the mind where its main objective is survival. When threatened, the mind reverts to its primitive actions such as eating or the fight-or-flight response. This is fine in a dangerous situation; however, daily, this only leads to dysfunction.

Finally, there is just allowing yourself to become comfortable in one state of mind. If you become comfortable thinking one way, you won't push yourself to think differently or do anything out of the ordinary. Even worse, you will feel you cannot think differently in the first place, so you will not try. If you can't break these patterns when necessary, you become trapped in this reduced mindset.

Apart from just not thinking, there are a few different ways people can intentionally sabotage critical thinking. You may have seen people use some of these negative strategies before, or maybe you have used them yourself in the past. These are ways people turn away from critical thinking and truthful arguments for falsehood and even manipulation. [17]

## Lack Of Respect For Reason

The reasoning is the cornerstone of critical thinking.

It is extremely important for forming sound arguments and deriving a conclusion from your premises and arguments. In everyday situations, people cannot accurately use critical thinking skills without a certain level of reasoning. [21]

As man's tool of understanding the world, it is necessary. It is the method of identifying entities through one's senses, integrating your perceptions into concepts, gaining knowledge through integration, integrating that knowledge into the rest of your knowledge, and finally evaluating and manipulating ideas and facts.

You can consider reasoning to be the process of thinking. Clarity defines reasoning rather than gut thinking or intuition. Also, clarity requires clear and identifiable building blocks. Additionally, the reasoning is an organized way of thinking as it is systematic and purposeful. It concentrates on the fundamentals of the argument and uses clear methods of logic and deduction to conclude. [21]

Knowing the importance of reasoning to sound thought patterns, it is no wonder that reasoning is so important to critical thinking. But what happens when someone does not have any respect for reasoning?

Suppose someone is making the argument that a severe storm is not about to take place. However, all logic points to a storm coming within minutes: it's dark, cloudy, the wind is blowing, and thunder and lightning have taken place.

Someone who lacks respect for reason would adamantly disagree. They support their argument by saying the clouds are just passing through, and thunder and lightning are not usually a sign of a storm. They continue to claim that a storm will not happen, even though all evidence points to a storm.

Their methods for reasoning quickly fall apart. There is no clarity in their argument. Instead of building an argument from the evidence around them or the concrete facts, they are making the argument based on vague premonitions.

Someone who does not have respect for reasoning refuses to see it in an argument. Because of this, they are not attempting to use critical thinking skills, which require a level of reasoning.

## Intellectual Arrogance

Intellectual arrogance is when people become full of themselves because of what they know. Sure, that person may be very smart, and that is fine, but when they have a pompous exaggerated view of their ability and knowledge because of their intelligence, which is when it becomes a problem. [5]

There are a few characteristics that signal someone who is intellectually arrogant: [5]

- They know they are the smartest person in the room and make it known that they think their opinions are the only ones that count.
- Most of the time, people will not tell them they are intellectually arrogant, and if they do, then the intellectually arrogant person will not believe them. They have to discover it on their own.
- Their recognition of their intellectual arrogance can lead to their downfall. Sustained success can give a person a feeling of infallibility or invincibility. Once that is gone, the person can feel lost.

Intellectual humility, however, is the opposite:

- These are the people who are smart enough to recognize that all ideas and opinions have some kind of value and that all issues and problems are multifaceted.

- They possess the ability to work as a group and do not put themselves above others.
- They do not rush to judge others.
- They try to elicit the best from every person they encounter.

A study revealed that a few characteristics that go along with a person who possesses an unhealthy amount of intellectual arrogance and how others evaluate them.

For one thing, they do not see themselves as others see them. They see themselves as exceedingly humble and would not dare to call themselves anything close to arrogant. However, other people who know them would think the exact opposite of that. They have seen the arrogance in full force from an outside lens and would say that this person is full of themselves.

Another thing found was in group projects, where

other team members gave better evaluations to those that they felt were humbler. Maybe the intellectually arrogant person contributed a lot to the project. Still, the way they felt that they were above everyone else in the group and the way they treated others made the rest of the group think little of them and would rather have worked with less arrogant people. [5]

Finally, people can usually agree on who is intellectually arrogant and who is intellectually humble, but it takes time. People will evaluate others genuinely based on evidence to support how they feel about them. If they spend only a short amount of time with someone, they do not have much time to conclude about that person. Sometimes, people may find it challenging to determine whether someone is humble or just shy, arrogant, or simply very extroverted.

You may have worked with someone who is intellectually arrogant. If not, you might encounter one someday. Imagine working on a group project. The intellectually arrogant one in the group thinks only their answers are right. They don't accept any opinions from the rest of the group. They try to appoint themselves the leader of the whole operation but do not take the suggestions of others on how things should get done. Their arguments are flawed because they do not listen to the reasoning of the other group members.

Therefore, intellectual arrogance completely derails critical thinking. Yes, critical thinkers are smart, but that is not their only characteristic. They are open-minded, unbiased, and open to new points of view. All of this takes a certain level of humility, and so the intellectually humble person makes for a better critical thinker.

## Unwillingness To Listen

This is the person who many people have

encountered at least once. The person who does not listen to what you are saying no matter what. They completely ignore your point of view in favor of their own because they do not agree, or they do not care to hear anything other than what they want to believe.

Someone unwilling to listen does not care to listen to reason, even if your argument is much more valid than their own. Their arguments are false, and they are fine with that. Either they know their argument is false, but they are too comfortable in that position to change it, or they are unaware they are wrong, but they have held that point of view for such a long time they do not care to listen to another one.

There are five key characteristics of bad listeners: [5]

**Interrupting**: This is probably the easiest to point out. Most people interrupt others, but only to a certain extent. With the person unwilling to listen, they constantly interrupt because they do not want to listen to what you have to say. Their own opinions are much more important to them because they feel that only they are correct.

**Closed-Mindedness**: People who don't want to listen to others are generally closed-minded. Their perspective is narrow, and it does not interest them in learning new ideas. Think of their worldview as a circle they are not willing to step outside of or expand.

**Too Busy**: With someone unwilling to listen, they might give their opinion, but when it is time for you to speak your mind, they say they are "too busy" to listen. They either turn their attention to their phone or some other distraction, or they may even just leave altogether. If they remain in front of you, you might get an occasional "uh-huh, sure" from them, but in reality, it focuses them on something else because they do not care to listen to what you have to say.

**Match Back**: This is when you can tell someone something, a serious story, or something that happened to you, but the person turns it around into something about themselves instead. They share something that happened to them that may or may not be similar to your own story and then try to give unsolicited advice on how they would have handled the situation. It is a way to make the situation more about them, so they don't have to listen to you.

Listening is an important aspect of critical thinking. On the one hand, it allows you to be open to other points of view. On another, you cannot properly evaluate someone's argument if you are not listening closely to what they are saying.

## Intellectual Laziness

Intellectual laziness goes hand-in-hand with passive thinking. This is when you are not thinking critically and not attempting to question statements from others. With intellectual laziness, people succumb to the social pressure of what other people around them believe and do not form opinions for themselves.

If there is a problem facing them, they go with the obvious answer, whether or not it is correct. It is the answer that stands out, and the first thing that catches their mind, so they go with it and do not look into the problem for what is correct. [10]

Suppose the intellectually lazy person normally follows a certain political view. They are extremely adamant about it and do not accept any outside view. Even if the opposite party says something that is, in fact, correct, the intellectually lazy person will not research for themselves to find that this person is correct, but will reject it just because it did not come from their party affiliation.

Another example is a person who has for their whole life believed that global warming is not happening.

They adamantly stick to that belief without taking the effort to research impartial sources to find out what is happening with climate change.

What often happens is that intellectually lazy people fall into the mindset that someone else cannot disagree with them. However, they are allowed to say whatever they want and offend, insult, and discredit that person for disagreeing with them. Essentially, they have convinced themselves of their own moral and intellectual superiority but are lazy because they refuse to take the time to consider any other point of view.

## Lack Of Respect For Evidence

In most cases, if the evidence presented to you supports your argument, then naturally, you can draw from it a conclusion that makes sense according to the argument. However, sometimes the evidence given to you is not entirely accurate, and this presents a challenge in determining what kind of conclusion you should be making.

This is where critical thinking comes in and why the use of evidence, and the respect of that evidence, is essential to good critical thinking skills. [16]

With evidence, such an important aspect of critical thinking, when a person does not take into account or respect the evidence presented to them and tries to conclude without recognizing any of the evidence in front of them, ultimately their argument and use of critical thinking skills fall apart. [16]

Imagine this scenario. It is Independence Day in the U.S., and fireworks are an essential part of the day. Your dog is afraid of fireworks, and your solution to the problem is not to launch fireworks in your yard this year. However, your brother argues that your dog will be fine and do fireworks anyway while ignoring the evidence that shows that your dog is afraid of them.

You point out that your dog doesn't like loud noises in general due to having a previous owner who shot fireworks and guns around them, leaving them afraid of similar loud noises. You also explain that last year you took your dog to a house where they shot fireworks, and the dog ran and hid. Even loud noises like sirens make your dog tremble.

Still, your brother does not respect the evidence presented to them about this and insist that their conclusion that fireworks on the 4th of July are necessary.

Based on the evidence you have found, the logical conclusion is that your dog, who you love very much, is afraid of fireworks, and you should not shoot them at your house because of this. However, because you ignored all of this evidence and your brother was adamant about sticking with his argument that celebrating the holiday requires fireworks, his argument does not present a logical conclusion in the case of your dog's fear.

# False Dichotomy

A false dichotomy is a type of logical fallacy. It is when only two choices are presented to you, although more exist. False dichotomy presents a spectrum of possible choices between two extremes. They are characterized by either "this or that" type of language or by the omission of choices

A false dichotomy involves people just seeing things in black and white terms without a wider perspective. They essentially say that if A is wrong, B must be the truth. This is another way that critical thinking derails because this thinking leads to the misinterpretation of pieces of evidence and reasons.

Typically, a dichotomy is a set of mutually exclusive, meaning that the alternatives overlap and mutually exhaustive, meaning there are other options, alternatives. Express with the words "like" or "or," the dichotomy does not imply extremes or that one option is better than the other. An example is: "Either this test is wrong, or the program is wrong."

However, the false dichotomy is not mutually exhaustive or mutually exclusive. The purpose is to force your opponent into an extreme position as the false dichotomy claims that there are only two positions for any situation.

Think of this example: "I thought you were a good person, but you were not in church today." This statement implies there are only two options; either you are a good person and go to church, or you are not a good person if you don't go to church.

Of course, there are several other options to consider. Suppose you attend church frequently, but you had a good reason to miss this one day. Another option would be that you follow another religion where you are not required to attend church, or you simply don't go to church in the first place. Neither of these options implies that you are a bad person either, but the false dichotomy leaves only two options to be considered.

A deductive argument, typical of a critical thinker, requires clarity and little room for alternative arguments. By the time we conclude a deductive argument, there should be no more questions remaining and no other options to consider.

For example, a deductive argument would say, "All men are mortal. Socrates was a man. Therefore, Socrates was mortal." This argument does not leave any room for alternative conclusions and does not leave any questions. The conclusion is definite, and there is no room for ambiguity.

A false dichotomy carries with it an underlying intolerance for ambiguity, but differently than a deductive argument. The false dichotomy carries with it the presumption that one answer or the other must be true, whether either is true or not. Usually, its purpose is to manipulate the argument in favor of the person making the argument. There is not much reasoning behind this as the deductive argument. Instead, there is an agenda behind it to reach the conclusion that the arguer wants.

Another example of a false dichotomy is, "If you want better schools, raise taxes. If you don't want your taxes raised, then you can't have better schools."

This situation implies there are only two solutions to the problem, higher taxes or bad schools. The intention behind it is clear, it makes it sound like if you do not pick the option of raising taxes, then you do not want better schools, and this makes you a bad person.

Several other solutions go along with improving schools, such as a change in school leadership, better use of resources, and hiring better teachers. But a false dichotomy comes with a certain intention or an inherent bias towards one option, and if you do not choose a certain option between the two extremes presented, then that makes you a bad person.

A common example of a false dichotomy is the saying, "You're either with me or against me." Again, this puts the person in front of you in a precarious situation where they need to decide between two extremes. Certainly, they care for you and want to be on your side, but if they disagree with you or if they choose not to be with you on this topic, that implies they do not care about you as much as they do.

# Inherited Opinion

Have you ever found that you believe something because your parents told you that as a child and seeing them act it out or talk about it all time reinforced the belief in you? Or maybe you learned something from a friend or a teacher, and for most of your life, you believed it. Finally, you took the time to research it for yourself and discovered everything to be completely untrue.

These opinions you have inherited often fall into the category of political opinions or religious opinions, things your parents probably followed, so naturally, you fell into this way of thinking as well. In other cases, they can be scientific facts, beliefs about the world around you, or beliefs about people different from you.

The inherited opinion is essentially believing something because someone else told you so. This is another factor that will sabotage critical thinking because it does not involve forming your own opinion based on your knowledge, experience, and reasoning. It is a form of passive thinking. Someone told you it was true, so you do not take it upon yourself to discover otherwise. [8]

Most of the time, inherited social factors influence opinions. Studies have found that in a lot of cases, certain social beliefs and long-held attitudes are largely the product of the social environment that a person grows up in. [8]

Things like knowledge of foreign affairs and political opinions are highly heritable actions and direct our choices for the kind of social niche we participate in, such as who we spend our time with and the activities that we partake in. [7]

Environmental factors and a person's individual experiences are strong determinants of a person's opinions and beliefs. However, there is little evidence to show there is necessarily a genetic component that contributes to certain attitudes. These tend to come from a person's personality and the way they grew up. [8]

As an example of inherited opinion, say you live in a small town in a rural part of the country. Others told you that the big city is bad. The people there are bad, they make poor choices, and their values and lifestyle are wrong. Additionally, they convinced you that the city itself is dirty and dangerous because of the crime that runs rampant there. Because of this, you grew up with the mindset that big cities are undesirable, and you want to stay away.

However, one day you are in the library, and you see a picture of New York City. The landmarks look cool, and the city itself seems quite beautiful. As she is passing by, the librarian tells you that she is from New York City, and she misses it and wants to go back. From there, you find yourself wondering if what others said about big cities was true.

Finally, you decide to find out for yourself. Despite the protests of your parents and the adults around you, you book a flight to New York. Once you get there, you are amazed. The city is even more beautiful in person. Although crowded and busy, you don't find it to be dangerous and dirty the way others informed you. The people you meet are also very kind and helpful.

From there, you change your opinion of big cities. You realize that the opinion you inherited from your parents was wrong and that the city is not as bad as they made it out to be.

Because you took it upon yourself to find out more about a big city, your opinion about it has completely changed. But what about someone who does not take it upon themselves to find out more beyond what they originally told them?

They don't go out of the way to learn more and broaden their perspective while eliminating their biases, all traits necessary for a critical thinker. They do not go out of their way to see what other people feel about a certain topic. Those with inherited opinions could find themselves with incorrect opinions on different beliefs, political, religious, and more, and they end up with unnecessary biases against different ethnicities and worldviews. They remain trapped inside their circle without trying to broaden their horizons.

Because of this, inherited opinions will sabotage critical thinking if the person with that opinion is a passive thinker and remains complacent in that form of thought.

Luckily there are a few ways to avoid inherited opinions.

**Evaluate Biases**: We know that bias completely ruins all critical thinking. You cannot form an objective opinion if you have some kind of bias in whatever situation you are trying to form an argument for. With inherited opinions, more than likely, you become biased due to the information given. However, the things you believed in your whole life are hard to put down, and it may be difficult to pinpoint exactly what these biases are. Think of particular topics that people have varied opinions on or topics that are controversial. Are there political, religious, or scientific opinions like climate change that you hold because someone around you holds the same opinion? Or maybe it can be something even simpler like what shows you like or what singers you think are good.

Thinking of your own biases is important, but it will also help to think of the biases that the people around you have. Does your grandparent make inappropriate comments about other people? Maybe your father is an adamant believer of conspiracy theories such as the Flat Earth Theory. Evaluate the biases of others to determine whether this is something you have picked up on.

**Fact Check**: Now that you are aware of the biases that you and those around you have, fact-check them. Do your research. Read books on the topic, research the history of it, and look at the news reports from a variety of sources to see various points of view. Speak to others who have a different opinion than yours. Join groups, whether in person or online, where people share different opinions on things.

Now that you have fact-checked these opinions start forming your own opinion on them. Follow the steps of critical thinking and draw your conclusions on these topics. Maybe you find that your opinion on the topic remains the same after doing your research and reasoning. This is fine; there is no requirement that your viewpoint has to change drastically. However, at least now, you have formed your opinion on it based on your thought patterns instead of following others.

**Tell Others**: Although you have changed your view on various topics based on facts and research, those around you have not. It's difficult to change the opinions of your parents, grandparents, or whoever you inherited your original opinion from, but it can't hurt to present facts and try, especially if they hold beliefs that are racist or just flat out wrong.

In addition to trying to inform the people who you inherited your opinion from, it would also be beneficial to tell others who are inheriting the same opinion, such as siblings or friends. Show them the research you have compiled and tell them your critical thinking skills you applied to come to your conclusion. Not only are you forming an opinion on your own, but you would also break the cycle for others.

# Process Of Critical Thinking

Like any thought strategy, there is a process that goes along with critical thinking. However, what you want to keep in mind about the critical thinking process is that although there are steps that go along with it, critical thinking is not necessarily a "technique." Rather, it is a state of mind.

A true critical thinker says to themselves, "I don't want to believe, I want to know." Critical thinking is intentional, it is specific, and the mental state the critical thinker is in is one that drives them to discover concrete information they can utilize in a practical sense. [6]

Critical thinking is the process of thinking about your thinking while you're thinking of making your thinking even better than it was before. There are two things crucial to the process of critical thinking and the state of mind that it entails.

One of them is that critical thinking is not just thinking, but a means for self-improvement. Not only does critical thinking entail a specific way of improving your thinking, but it also requires skills such as constant learning and broadening your perspective on life, which benefits you in other areas of your life. [6]

Another thing is that the self-improvement that you gain from critical thinking comes from skill in using the standards by which you would appropriately assess your thinking. In other words, it is self-improvement in terms of your thinking through standards that assess your thinking.

Another reason that critical thinking involves such a specific state of mind is that it involves putting certain restraints on your thinking through intellectual standards. So, to raise the standard of thinking to a higher level, you are essentially using a method of thinking that is not familiar to you, such as a spontaneous thought or gut thinking where you're just going along with the first thing that comes to your mind. It's about making your brain work harder to raise your standards and improve your thought patterns altogether.

There are a set of basic steps that make up the critical thinking process, and the more you use them, the sharper your critical thinking skills will be. These steps are:

**Reconstructing the Situation**: This involves breaking the situation down to its most basic form. Put it in the simplest words you can understand it in. Break down the argument into its basic premises and conclusion. Determine how they fit together. Ask questions about the evidence.

**Revealing Hidden Issues**: These would include bias and manipulation. Does the person making the argument fall into any of the traps that sabotage critical thinking, such as inherited opinions or intellectual arrogance? Or do they use certain fallacies like false dichotomy? Also, determine what the intention behind making this argument is. Are they genuinely trying to inform, or are they trying to manipulate the situation, so they come out on top?

**Making the Best Decision**: This is where you draw your conclusion to the situation. At this stage, keep in mind that rather than choosing an answer because it feels right, you should subject all options to scrutiny and skepticism. Passive thinkers choose the first answer that they think sounds right. Critical thinkers take all the possibilities because the conclusion that seems the most correct could end up being very wrong upon further examination.

Critical thinking is a set of different skills that has some core skills, like applying skepticism, but also has a variety of other skills that vary between individuals.

One of those skills is communication. There are two types of communication that people engage in. One of them is just surface-level communication or trivial communication. This communication doesn't require any kind of education or any real in-depth thinking. Think of it as small talk or gossip, things that don't utilize any skills to do it well. This kind of communication isn't all that deep. [6]

The other communication is the type that results in a deep, in-depth conversation. It involves the four modalities of reading, writing, speaking, and listening. Sometimes they can be used all together, or sometimes they can be used separately, but all of them require some higher level of thinking and effort. These four things involve problem-solving and critical thinking skills throughout the entire process.

You can think of communication as a transaction

between two logics. For example, in reading, there is the logic of the author and the logic of the reader. The reader reconstructs the logic of the author into their own experience, and they evaluate it on their own. There is a similar process for writing, speaking, and listening.

Another skill important to critical thinking is collaborative learning. Collaborative learning becomes useful when it is grounded in disciplined critical thinking. How many times have you been in a group setting where you had to work on a project or solve a problem together, but people weren't taking it seriously, and group members were displaying actions that sabotage critical thinking such as intellectual arrogance and not listening. Surely not much got done on the project, or the quality of the completed project was not very good. [6]

But if you are in a situation where everyone works hard together, everyone puts forward the effort to follow the steps of critical thinking and puts together conclusions and arguments that are sound, valid, and grounded in reason; the result is very different.

Without critical thinking, collaborative learning turns into collaborative mislearning. It's just a collection of bad thinking thrown together in a messy way that does not yield any positive results, and bad thinking becomes validated among the group.

Some examples of collaborative learning are prejudices, stereotypes, and mass hysteria. They stem from a group of people engaged in bad thinking practices, and they validate them amongst themselves.

However, when disciplined critical thinking is present in a collaborative learning-setting, you get a mode of collaboration that is grounded in education, knowledge, and insight.

Curiosity goes hand-in-hand with critical thinking. For curiosity to flourish, there must evolve from disciplined inquiry and reflection. Left to itself, your curiosity will wander, leading you into unhelpful, and at worst dangerous, situations. [6]

Intellectual curiosity is different. Here you are still allowing your mind to wander but in a controlled way. It involves intellectual humility, intellectual courage, intellectual integrity, intellectual perseverance, and faith in reason. Intellectual curiosity proves its value because it leads to knowledge, understanding, and insight. It can also help to broaden, deepen, and sharpen our minds, making us better, more humane, and more richly endowed people.

You have to be more than curious to reach these means, though. You have to be willing to work, willing to suffer through confusion and frustration, willing to face limitations and overcome obstacles, be open to the views of others, and be willing to entertain ideas that many people find threatening.

One final skill that goes along with critical thinking is self-esteem. You might think self-esteem is not very important to your thinking process, but it plays a big role. Healthy self-esteem comes from a justified sense of self-worth, and self-worth comes from your level of perceived competence, ability, and genuine success. [6]

However, there is a healthy self-esteem useful to critical thinking skills, and there is an unhealthy version. If a person feels good about themselves for no particular reason other than they are full of themselves, that misplaced sense of self-worth clouds their judgment, and they fall into the trap of intellectual arrogance.

But if you just have a good sense of self and feel good

about the person you are, you will find yourself more confident in your ability to reason soundly. You will find yourself more confident with your conclusion after following all the steps of critical thinking.

It is the variety of skills between individuals that explains the need for peer review, between different individuals. One person might be good at timing logic, but another person may be good at mathematical logic and another person good at data assessment and so on.

## Formulate Your Question

The critical thinking process is essential for solving problems, especially with ill-defined problems. These types of problems are those that are complex and do not have an obvious answer or an expected solution. Although there is no correct answer to the problems, using the process of critical thinking, you can come to a solution that is reasonable and valid.

These types of problems are the kind that requires a systematic approach, one that critical thinking is perfect for. Without this systematic approach, it will be more difficult or even impossible to reach a satisfactory conclusion that makes sense. So, to achieve the best results for whatever solution you are trying to find, you must follow the steps in the critical thinking process in order and carry them out thoroughly as all the steps are necessary to reach a sound conclusion. [31]

The first step in the critical thinking process is to formulate your question. This will help you to clarify the problem at hand.

To take a situation as an example, imagine you have decided you want to live a healthier lifestyle, and one of the steps you will take in achieving your goal is joining a gym. There are two gyms close to you. You need to choose one, and both come with their pros and cons.

So, the question is, how do you make the best decision?

One of the most important parts of this step is knowing what you are looking for and explaining it in detail to formulate a detailed question. Layout a list of criteria for you to make your decision. In this case of choosing between two different gyms to join, some things you might look for are the distance from home, how big it is, the amenities they offer, and how friendly the people are.

Knowing what you are looking for in solving a problem through critical thinking is an essential first step. A detailed question will guide you as you move forward in the process. [31]

## Gather Your Information

The next step in solving a problem through critical thinking is to gather all of your information. Information gathering helps you to weigh out the different options presented to you, moving closer to a decision that hits your goal.

Gather as many details as you can about the situation. These include the pros and cons, practical information, and questions you have about the situation. Explore any judgments, arguments, opinions, and conclusions that you can find about the issue, whether this is looking online, reading it in a book, or speaking directly with others. Ask yourself what evidence you can find that will back up or maybe disprove your experience, beliefs, or opinions on the topic. [31]

Think of this phase as going through analysis and interpretation of the information you have gathered.

Also, at this step, you should be able to clarify the problem or situation and ensure you clearly understand the issue you are trying to find a critical solution for. Ask the five W's and H questions (who, what, when, where, why, and how) to refine your thoughts on the issue. Some of these might include what is happening, who is involved, what are the stakes in the process, and what is the best way to characterize, categorize, or classify this?

To be even more thorough, go into a deeper analysis of the matter at hand. Consider other perspectives, beliefs, assumptions, and opinions apart from your own. Do this with an open mind so you can consider as many options as possible. You should also analyze all the facts and any metrics available to corroborate the evidence.

Some questions you can ask are: what are you claiming, why do you think a certain way, what are the arguments (pros and cons), what assumptions must you make to accept that conclusion, what is your basis for saying that, what are the underlying or hidden issues, and what would success look like to all the people involved in the problem? [31]

Going into the example of trying to find a gym to join, find answers to the details you considered when formulating your question.

You find that Gym 1 is a few miles closer to your house, which would give you a more convenient commute. While Gym 1 is closer, Gym 2 has more amenities such as a few group exercise studios, a spinning studio, a pool, and a sauna. Naturally, Gym 2 is more expensive, but it offers more. However, Gym 1 has a robust schedule of group exercise classes you are very interested in.

As part of gathering information, look at some pictures and reviews online, talk to people who attend the gym, and even ask for a tour.

Be as thorough as possible about gathering information because it will inform your answers in the next step.

## Apply The Information

This is the stage when all the information you found on the topic comes together. At the formulating a question phase and the gathering information stage, you can consider the "Presentation of the Problem" part of solving a problem through critical thinking. Now, to apply the information phase, we can consider this the "Taking Action" phase of the process.

This is where you consider your reasoning and formulate a conclusion to the situation. Additionally, you will try to evaluate the validity of your argument and solution.

At this phase, this is where you identify and secure the elements needed to draw a reasonable conclusion. Here, you will compile all the data, statements, principles, evidence, beliefs, and opinions from the previous phases and brainstorm ideas. At this point, you will identify possible conclusions and determine the viability of the conclusion you come up with. [31]

At this phase, there are going to be critical questions you will want to ask yourself before coming to a definite conclusion on the issue.

Some of these are what conclusions can we draw given what I know, what can I rule out, what does this evidence imply, what additional information do I need to resolve this question, what are the consequences of doing things that way, what are some alternatives I haven't yet explored, and are there any undesirable consequences that I can and should foresee? [31]

At this phase in selecting a gym example, here you want to put together all the information you have gathered so far and come to a solution on it. Consider what would ultimately be best for you in this situation. Is distance a bigger concern for you, or is it the expense? Would you rather be at a gym with a greater selection of group exercise classes, or do you want other types of amenities? Also, consider the other information you gathered, such as the reviews and speaking to others.

## Consider The Implications

In the last step, you have come up with a solution to the problem at hand, but it is not enough to just settle on the first conclusion you come up with. Critical thinking in problem-solving goes way beyond that.

At this phase, it is time to consider the long-term effects of your decision. Perhaps right now, it seems right, but what consequences will it have in years to come? This is the thing you want to think about before you settle with your decision permanently.

This is all about assessing the credibility of the solution you came up with by applying the information. Here, you want to review any new evidence and ideas generated since you came up with your solution. Evaluate with fresh eyes the validity of the possible solution and probe for weaknesses in your thinking and logic. [31]

In this phase, some questions you can ask yourself are how credible is the claim, how strong are the arguments, do we have your facts right, how confident can we be in your conclusion given what you now know, what are the consequences of this solution, what would it look like in a year if you implemented this solution?

A strategy you can take to guide the process of

considering the implications is to start by recapping the critical thinking process, possible solutions, and how you arrived at them. Think of any flaws that could have been present in your reasoning. Was there any bias in making the decision? Did you pass over or leave or any important information? [31]

Finally, use the above questions to evaluate the validity of your argument or solution. If you can answer positively to most or all of the questions, then it is safe to say that the implications will not have any significant negative effects on you.

If you cannot answer positively to most of the questions, then it is time to backtrack and reevaluate your critical thinking process. This could mean that you need to gather more information or correct information. It could also mean that you need to refine your question better, thus, returning to the beginning of the process.

In the case of the gym example, suppose you went with Gym 1. What implications will it have on you in the future? It is closer to home and not as expensive as Gym 2, so it will have a better effect on you financially in the long run. It is not as big as Gym 2, and while this may be fine for now, will you find yourself wanting to be around more people and in bigger group exercise classes in the future?

## Explore Other Points Of View

After you have considered the implications of your conclusion, the critical work is still not finished as you want to be completely sure you are making the right choice.

This final phase is a chance for you to take a step out of the situation and look at it as a neutral person. Think of this as a moment to explore other alternatives to what you have come up with and see if you can come up with something better.

This step involves speaking to or reading about others who have a different point of view than you. One of the core aspects of critical thinking is being open-minded and able to explore other perspectives. This is very important for figuring out whether the decision you made is the best one and if there is a better one out there that someone else has come to that might fit you better. You might also determine that you can combine someone else's conclusion with yours to make an even stronger one.

In the case of choosing a gym, suppose you decided the answer to your question is that Gym 1 is the best solution for you and your lifestyle at this point. However, it might still be beneficial to you to revisit Gym 2. Take one more look at the perspective of people that go to that gym and find out what makes them happy there. It can help you to determine whether Gym 1 would be the best answer for you or not.

You might even consider other workout options such as other gyms that you might not have looked at or alternative fitness areas like community centers, the fitness center at your housing complex, or even working out from home.

In many cases, solutions made from critical thinking do not just involve a choice between two answers. You might find that one of the two answers is best for you, but then realize there are several other solutions out there to explore, and it might take more digging to come to the solution to your problem.

Before coming to your final decision, take the time to narrow down your decision and ensure that this is truly the best decision you can come to before settling on your solution completely. Take the time to question, confirm, validate, and connect your reasoning to your results.

Ask yourself if you can be more precise on your choice, how good was your methodology, and how well did you follow it. How good is your evidence, and is there anything that you were missing before you committed to the decision.

Following this process of critical thinking carefully, it will better equip you to make well-thought-out decisions on complex and ill-defined problems. Although sometimes it can seem like with some problems we face, critical thinking is unnecessary; it is something we use every day in either complex choices or issues that do not seem as complex such as selecting a gym to join.

# Can Critical Thinking Be Learned?

At some point in your life, you may have heard about how important critical thinking is. For many people, their first encounter with critical thinking comes in school, where a lot of the lessons have to do with critical thinking in some capacity. Some may say it is one of the most valuable skills that we expect students to learn in school. Outside of school, we prize critical thinking skills among employers and academics.

Although many praise critical thinking skills, are these skills learnable? In some ways, yes and in some ways, no.

What we know so far about critical thinking is that it is more of a frame of mind rather than a process or technique that can be learned and includes cognitive and affective domains of reasoning. Cognition is the set of all mental abilities and processes such as attention, memory, judgment, evaluation, problem-solving, and decision making, and affective domains of reasoning, meaning our motivations, perceptions, attitudes, and values. So critical thinking is a set of skills, knowledge, and attitudes rather than a set of cognitive skills all on its own. [26]

Because of this, while critical thinking is an important thing to teach, educators often struggle with teaching critical thinking skills because critical thinking has many aspects difficult to evaluate, and not everyone has them. Additionally, a lot of students find themselves challenged by tasks requiring critical thought, despite educators attempting to teach them. For example, students good at learning through memorization will struggle when expected to use their judgment to reach conclusions on their own. [26]

Although outside institutions call on schools to do a better job at teaching critical thinking, it ends up being a lot more difficult than it would seem from the outside. Studies conducted over the last 30 years have shown that numerous students are ill-equipped in their critical thinking skills. [30]

It remains difficult to teach because it is not a skill like riding a bike or solving a math problem that has a very distinct step-by-step process. While we can break critical thinking down into steps, the process of thinking intertwines with the content of thought or knowledge base. Thus, if you tell a student to look at an issue from a variety of perspectives, if they are unaware of other perspectives, then they can't think of it that way. You can teach about how people ought to think, but if they don't have the background knowledge, then they cannot easily implement the advice.

Consider what we can call surface thinking. We interpret anything you hear and read by considering what you already know about similar subjects. Your background knowledge of any subject allows you to interpret it in the best way that you can and come to your conclusion. Background knowledge also tends to narrow your perspective on the subject as you dive into it deeper because your mind assumes the new information is related to what you've just been thinking about. [30]

With deep knowledge, you can penetrate that surface thinking to find deeper meaning in what you are hearing or reading, which can allow you to expand your critical thinking skills. When someone is more aware of the information presented in an argument or problem, the ability to solve it comes much easier.

While already knowing about the subject is important, it is not the only strategy. It is also about the ability to look for information that you do not already know. Knowing when to seek new information will serve to expand your knowledge base for not only the situation at hand but future problems as well. [30]

We can assist this by making connections between similar problems faced in the past. If you had a problem with weeds growing in your garden that you had solved before and a similar situation appears later, you can refer back to that last issue with the weeds and see if there was anything you did there that can help now. Regulating your thoughts and making connections is called metacognition.

While people cannot teach critical thinking directly through basic instruction, practicing the skills mentioned above can improve your critical thinking. [30] There are a few strategies you can repeatedly perform to acquire important critical thinking skills. [19]

**Attempt to Understand**: In all honesty, critical thinking is a difficult skill, and the best way to learn how to do it is through the easiest means and working your way up from there. One of the first things you can do is read or listen intending to understand. A lot of times, we read or listen to something/someone with the objective of pleasure. To practice critical thinking, do it with the intent of understanding what exactly it is that you are learning.

**Practice**: Practice makes perfect, and that is especially true with critical thinking. The best way to strengthen critical thinking skills is through constantly practicing all the while being deliberate and intentional in what you are doing.

**Transferring Skills**: Although you may know how to solve problems in one area, such as through writing, it does not mean you know how to apply those skills in a different area, such as science.

**Gain Practical Knowledge**: You can read about a topic as much as you want, but experiencing it for yourself is just as valuable. Having a practical understanding and knowledge of an area can help you think more critically about it. Suppose you are very knowledgeable about art but do not know much beyond the theory of it. It would be helpful to go out and experience it, whether that is viewing art exhibitions, seeing artists at work, or becoming involved in creating art yourself.

**Map Out Arguments**: This can be a good way to facilitate critical thinking before you start getting the hang of it. It can make a high-level and abstract concept seem much easier to follow.

**Be Aware of Your Beliefs**: As we know, beliefs can influence critical thinking and sometimes inhibit critical thinking skills. Often, we seek information that confirms our beliefs rather than confronts different points of view. Know how your beliefs might influence your critical thinking and try to overcome them by thinking objectively.

We all need to improve and refine the thinking

process, to think more effectively. This includes brainstorming without edits, making mistakes, finding the "easy" solutions, and then assimilating them to grow, improve, learn, and ultimately change your thinking. [19]

Ask questions whenever you discover or discuss new information — remember the who, what, where, when, why, how questions. Exercise your critical thinking skills in everyday life, starting with simple problems and topics, and soon you find that critical thinking comes much more naturally to you.

# What Is The Best Time To Learn Critical Thinking?

Learning critical thinking can start at any age. There is no limit on how young or old you have to be to learn critical thinking. Anyone is capable of acquiring and enhancing their critical thinking skills.

However, the ideal time to learn critical thinking is when you are young. Learning science and critical thinking should start early. This way, it becomes a habit that children carry with them into their adult life that they improve as they get older.

Children are capable of various learning capacities at different stages in their life. A study conducted by French psychologist Jean Piaget, in his theory on the cognitive development of children, concluded there are four main stages of cognitive development in the early stages of childhood development.

- **Sensorimotor Stage** - From birth to age two, children learn about the world through their senses and manipulation of objects.

- **Preoperational Stage** - From ages two through seven, they are developing memory and imagination and understanding things symbolically, such as the idea of the past and future.

- **Concrete Operational Stage** - From ages seven through eleven, they become more aware of external events and feelings other than their own.

- **Formal Operational Stage** - From age eleven, up to when children can use logic to solve problems, view the world around them, and plan for their future. [1]

The Formal Operational Stage is also the ideal time to begin ensuring children learn critical thinking skills.

But just because children are capable of starting to practice critical thinking skills at the age of eleven, this does not mean everyone starts with the same level of skills. This is because, even from a young age, people have different levels of cognitive strengths, such as how some people are better at memory than logic and reasoning. [1]

Although people start with different levels of cognitive strengths, this does not mean cognitive skills cannot improve. There are a couple of different ways to help strengthen cognitive skills in a child.

To improve weak cognitive skills, the first step to take on the road to improvement is first identifying what skills the child is weak in through a cognitive assessment, which takes a deep look at how the child performs cognitively and identifies strengths and weaknesses.

After that, one of the ways you can strengthen weak skills is by applying cognitive training (brain training). This uses fun and challenging mental

exercises to target and improve weak cognitive skills.
[1]

One of those important aspects of critical thinking that children are starting to develop is determining the validity or credibility of a source. Determination of whether young children are capable of such differentiation has been the cause of debate. Still, researchers have shown that children as young as three and four years old already have some sense of individuals differing in their credibility. [33]

At this age, they become aware that people around them are capable of making misleading statements. They come to understand the possibility of deception around their preschool years. Although the idea of a fallacy or a false dichotomy is lost, they understand that appearances and reality can diverge, that people may hold false beliefs, and that verbal statements might not reflect actual beliefs.

It is important to start strengthening critical thinking skills as soon as possible because cognitive skills have an impact on whether people are successful or whether they struggle in thinking and learning.

Since the basis of critical thinking is how people think as opposed to what people think, there are a few ways to begin shaping how a child thinks and, therefore, strengthen their critical thinking skills as soon as possible: [34]

**Ask Open-Ended Questions**: These kinds of questions ensure the child has to think about the answer before responding. You can ask yes or no questions, but they don't call for a very deep response. Instead, ask, "why do you feel this way?" or "why do you like this?" These encourage the child to respond creatively without having to worry about giving the right or wrong answer.

**Categorize and Classify**: Classification requires

identification and sorting according to some set of rules, which is a good skill for a child to learn. Getting them involved with a classification activity now and then allows them to discover, understand, and apply these skills. Classification activities can be anything from sorting laundry to book titles.

**Work in Groups**: This allows children to understand the thought processes of their peers and discover multiple ways of approaching a problem. It is good practice for working together with others later in life, setting up arguments and premises, and cultivating open-mindedness.

**Let Them Make Decisions**: It might be useful to help them consider the pros and cons of a situation at this age, but you can let them make the final decision on their own and help them evaluate the decision later.

It is imperative to get everyone to think rationally

from an early age. This would solve the world's problems in a lot of ways. In teaching the skills and characteristics of critical thinking as early as possible, it eliminates much of the possibility for closed-mindedness, bias, and inherited opinions, which lead to issues such as racism and intolerance.

# Critical Thinking Vs. Overthinking

Imagine finding yourself in a problem at work where you have difficulty expanding the exposure of your product. This is a prime example of a situation where following the steps of critical thinking will be beneficial from forming the groundwork of creating a question, gathering information, and analyzing that information.

But instead of following through with the critical thinking process, the more you think of the problem at hand, you get anxious. You think about what could happen if you don't figure out how to solve the problem promptly: people will stop buying, you won't be able to reach enough people, and your business will eventually have to shut down.

Even when you come up with solutions to the problem, no matter how sound, you question those solutions until you feel like they wouldn't have worked out anyway, and the whole process continuously falls apart. You spend a lot of time on it, but find it harder and harder to come up with solutions.

This is a prime example of overthinking. In a critical thinking situation, you would work through the process in a controlled and organized way. With overthinking, all signs of structure fall away, anxiety creeps in, and your productivity is gone.

There is a crucial difference between overthinking and critical thinking. Overthinking has overtones of obsessing about a subject, usually someone else's behavior but often your own. You keep replaying what happened in your head as if you're trying to understand it, but the problem is that you're not trying to understand it. You're judging it, and you ask questions designed to show that someone is right and someone else is wrong.

With overthinking, you end up spending a lot more time thinking about a problem than you should, but that does not mean it is productive thinking. Critical thinking is productive. It gets things done; it solves problems promptly, and it is organized and is free of any biases. Overthinking, however, wastes time and mental energy. [23]

In critical thinking, you are actively looking for a solution to the problem, developing steps you can take to reach a conclusion. There are certain strategies and skills you can employ to reach the desired solution. Because critical thinking involves such careful thought, it helps to decrease stress.

Overthinking, on the other hand, does not use a strategy. It involves ruminating, worrying, and over-analyzing. With overthinking, you will find yourself dwelling on a problem rather than finding a viable solution. Because of this, it increases stress, and the more stressed you feel, the more likely you are to focus on the negative aspects of the situation. This creates an ongoing loop of anxiety, and critical thinking becomes lost. [23]

Overthinking isn't productive; it's destructive. It stalls you, prevents you from moving forward. Critical thinking, however, is all about seeking to understand. It involves no judgment. You ask questions designed to elicit useful information. Questions that bring you closer to a deeper understanding. [23]

Studies have shown that focusing on negative events can be the biggest predictor of major mental health problems such as depression and anxiety. Part of the reason overthinking causes so much stress is because you are listening to that inner voice critical of yourself and telling you that you are wrong or inadequate. This leads you to overthink situations. [2]

The next time you overthink instead of critical thinking, there are a few strategies you can try to reel your mind back in. Then you can put forward more of a calm and collected mindset and start putting into process your critical thinking skills. [2]

**Stand Up to Your Negative Inner Voice**: Your inner negative voice perpetuates your overthinking by making you more anxious as it goes on. To stop your negative inner voice from taking hold of you, first, take note of what that inner voice tells you when it comes up. Then think about where these words are coming from. Does it have to do with a current situation such as work or someone you love? Or did it start from an earlier life event that left you feeling inadequate as an adult? After you understand where it is coming from, you can separate it from your more positive thoughts. Finally, whenever those negative thoughts come back, push it away. You can do this by coming up with a set of phrases that talk back to the inner voice, such as, "I can do this" and "I am capable of solving my problems."

**Choose Your Thoughts with Mindfulness**: An effective way to stop overthinking, thinking with mindfulness, is about learning to control or focus your attention to increase calmness and self-awareness. This way, you are better able to understand and have control over your behavior.

**Change the Way You See Problems**: Instead of facing problems with stress and ruminating in a negative issue, change the way you see and approach the problems you encounter. Instead of seeing a challenge as something bad, think of it as a positive challenge that you will be stronger for overcoming. Accept that you have a lot of control over your circumstances by having a positive mindset. Commit to overcoming these challenges to feel powerful and proactive in the face of them.

# Conclusion

Critical thinking is essential for analyzing information and coming to clear and sound conclusions to any argument you make or any solution to a problem. It requires a process that includes examining evidence and making your judgments about whatever it is you are thinking about.

As important as critical thinking is, avoid things such as intellectual arrogance, not listening, and being quick to judge or else your whole argument for thinking critically falls apart just as fast as it began.

There are endless situations where you can use critical thinking. Looking back, you were probably in a situation that involved critical thinking without even realizing it. However, it is important to understand that it is how you use your critical thinking skills that determine the effectiveness of it.

Above all, critical thinking is a state of mind that not everyone possesses naturally. Although schools attempt to teach critical thinking, it takes consistent practice to train your brain to think critically at any time.

As with anything, you should strive to be the best thinker that you can be. Better critical thinking skills will enable you to face any situation head-on and solve problems with accuracy and efficiency. No matter where you are, in work, in school, or in everyday life situations, you find that critical thinking is necessary.

Despite the numerous techniques and skills that come with critical thinking, the best thing you can do for yourself is practice. Practice every critical thinking strategy, take on all the characteristics of a good thinker, and actively monitor yourself to ensure you are avoiding anything and everything that serves to ruin good critical thinking.

# References

[1]  "4 Cognitive States For Child Development." *Learning Rx.*

[2]  "Are You Overthinking Everything?" *PsychAlive.*

[3]  Ash, Eve. "Five characteristics of bad listeners." (2017). *Smart Company.*

[4]  Bailyn, Evan. "The Value of Active Critical Thinking." (2012). *Early Writings of Evan Bailyn.*

[5]  Baylor University. "People with higher 'intellectual arrogance' get better grades." (2015). *Science Daily.*

[6]  "Critical Thinking: Basic Questions & Answers." *The Foundation For Critical Thinking.*

[7]  Barber, Nigel. "What Behaviors Do We Inherit via Genes?" (2015). *Psychology Today.*

[8]  DeAnelis, Tori. "Are beliefs inherited?" (2004). *APA.*

[9]  "Deductive and Inductive Arguments." Internet Encyclopedia of Philosophy.

[10]  Dwyer, Christopher. "5 Barriers to Critical Thinking." (2019). Psychology Today."

[11]  Gambrill, Peter. "Effective Argumentation: Premises and Conclusions." *San José State University.*

[12]  Girard, Patrick. "Good and bad arguments." *University of Auckland.*

[13]  "Good and bad arguments." *Acrewoods.*

[14]  Hasa. "What are Premises and Conclusions in an Argument." (2016). Pediaa.

[15]  Haplin, John. "Ampliative Reasoning and Informal Logic." (2010). The Logic Cafe.

[16]  Horowitz, Sophie. Sliwa, Paulina. "Respecting all the evidence." (2015). *Springer Science+Business Media Dordrecht.*

[17]  Hurson, Tim. (2007). *Think Better: An Innovator's Guide to Productive Thinking.*

[18]  "Is it rational to trust your gut feelings? A Neuroscientist explains." (2018). *The Conversation.*

[19]  Kaminske, Althea Need. "Can We Teach Critical Thinking?" (2019). *Learning Scientists.*

[20]  Lau, Joey Y. F. (2011). *An Introduction to Critical Thinking and Creativity.*

[21]  Landauer, Jeff. Rowlands, Joseph. "Reason." (2001). *Importance of Philosophy.*

[22]  Moore, B. N., & Parker, R. (1989). *Critical thinking: evaluating claims and arguments in everyday life.*

[23]  Morin, Amy. "Problem-Solving Is Helpful. Overthinking Is Harmful. Here's How to Tell the Difference." (2019). *Thrive Global.*

[24]  Nordquist, Richard. "Premise Definition and Examples in Arguments." (2019). Thought Co.

[25]  O'Neil, William J. "Intuitive and Non-Intuitive Thinking." (1988). *How to Make Money in Stocks—A Winning System in Good Times or Bad.*

[26]  Pennetieri, Regina C. "Can Critical Thinking Skills Be Taught?" (2015). *Radiology Technology.*

[27]  "Our Concept and Definition of Critical Thinking." (2019). *The Foundation For Critical Thinking.*

[28]  Sieck, Winston. "Critical Thinking in Everyday Life." *Thinker Academy.*

[29]  "Some Advice on How to Learn Critical Thinking." (2019). *A Research Guide For Students.*

[30]  Willingham, Daniel T. "Critical Thinking: Why Is It So Hard to Teach?" (2007). *American Educator.*

[31]  "A Systematic Process For Critical Thinking." *University of Florida.*

[32]  Elder, Linda. Paul, Richard. "Critical Thinking Development: A Stage Theory." *The Foundation For Critical Thinking.*

[33]  Heyman, Gail D. "Children's Critical Thinking When Learning From Others." (2008). *US National Library of Medicine National Institutes of Health.*

[34]  "Think About It: Critical Thinking." *Scholastic.*

# The Art Of Critical Thinking

## How To Build The Sharpest Reasoning Possible For Yourself

By

Christopher Hayes

# Introduction

Critical thinking is a way to improve your quality of thinking through rational and unbiased evaluation of factual evidence. We use these skills every day, and they are extremely important in many daily situations.

As a beginner in critical thinking, it can be hard to know where to start. Some of the questions you might have are when can I use critical thinking, how do I practice it, and why would it be useful to me in the first place?

However, once you understand the basics of critical thinking, the building blocks of creating arguments, and are aware of the things that serve to derail critical thinking completely, you can begin to apply it to everyday life.

Once you know how to utilize the processes of critical

thinking in real-time, you will see immense benefits to your life and will find that your thought processes become more efficient and organized.

As a researcher who makes a conscious effort to use critical thinking strategies as often as possible and understands the immense benefits it has to the quality of life, I am here to help you learn ways to improve your critical thinking skills.

Critical thinking makes your life easier. It helps you to make better, more informed decisions whether you are buying a car, a house, choosing which university to attend, or something as simple as choosing a gym to become a member of. If you begin to practice critical thinking daily, it becomes easier, and you can begin to apply it to any situation that you find yourself in.

This book will tell you everything you need to know about applying critical thinking skills to your daily life. Not only will you learn exactly why critical thinking is essential for you to learn, but you will also find skills and strategies that you can practice every day to become a master thinker.

You might be thinking that critical thinking is too complicated, and you will not be able to remember all of those techniques and use them in your everyday life. However, if you take it seriously and make a commitment to implementing critical thinking into your life, you will start to see some changes.

Like everything, it takes practice, but fortunately, there are ways to break it down into easy steps.

You must remember that critical thinking is more of a mindset than a set technique. Before you know it, you will find yourself wondering why you ever found it difficult in the first place, but you won't get there if you wait any longer. Every moment you hesitate is a moment where critical thinking could have benefitted you.

You want to make changes in your life. You want to think in a way that is clear and organized, and you want to make the best decisions for yourself. Don't hesitate a moment longer, and find out how you can become a critical thinker now.

# Importance Of Being A Critical Thinker

Often, when people think of critical thinking, they picture using it in a classroom setting or at work on a major project. However, critical thinking is so much more than that. People use critical thinking skills every day, and it is vital to everyday life.

Critical thinking leads us to unlock our intellectual independence. By doing so, it moves people away from rushed conclusions, mystification, and reluctance to question received wisdom, tradition, and authority. It also moves people towards intellectual discipline, a clear expression of ideas, and acceptance of personal responsibility for your thinking.

Considered to be the ability to think clearly and rationally about what to do or what to believe, critical thinking also includes one's ability to engage and reflect on situations. Most importantly, critical thinkers can engage in independent thinking. With this, they can form opinions by themselves through their perceptions and research instead of relying on others to form their opinions for them.

When a person takes the time to build their critical thinking skills, there are a few things that they can do that non-critical thinkers (passive thinkers) can't do or can't do very easily. These include: [4]

- Understanding logical connections between ideas.
- The ability to identify, construct, and evaluate arguments for themselves.
- Detect inconsistencies in reasoning.
- Solve problems using a systematic approach.
- Reflect on the justification of the beliefs and values that they possess.

Knowledge is essential to critical thinking. This includes specific and general knowledge. The more you know about a topic, the more you will be able to think critically about it. However, critical thinking is about more than just accumulating knowledge. It is more about what you can do with that knowledge. A person can know everything in existence, but if they do not know how to apply what they have learned, and then it is useless.

While forming arguments is another essential aspect of critical thinking, this does not mean that critical thinkers become callous and like to fight or be critical of other people. It revolves around improving theories, playing a role in constructive tasks, and overcoming fallacies and other flawed arguments. It is also useful for improving work processes, social institutions, and creative ideas.

The true importance of critical thinking, however, comes down to a few reasons.

**It Enhances Language and Communication Skills**: Critical thinking plays a key role in how people communicate with each other. A lot of times, we may not realize it at the moment. Still, the next time you are having an in-depth conversation with someone or giving a presentation, pay attention to your thought processes, what about it would you consider critical thinking and how you can improve those thought processes for next time.

Critical thinking serves to improve how people form and express their ideas vastly. It allows your mind to take the time to analyze and craft your ideas before expressing them clearly and concisely. It helps you to form well-developed arguments that are valid, strong, concise, and cogent, as well as creating strong premises that lead to supported conclusions. These processes are essential to think through your ideas and effectively communicating with those around you.

Additionally, critical thinking improves comprehension abilities. If you are reading something new and quite difficult to process, critical thinking is what allows you to analyze the logical structure of the text and help you to comprehend the knowledge better.

**It Promotes Creativity**: Critical thinking and creativity go hand in hand. Critical thinking involves thinking clearly and rationally, following the rules of logic and scientific reasoning. However, creativity involves coming up with new and useful ideas as well as alternative possibilities. The two of them work together in the way that creativity is necessary to solve problems; however, critical thinking is essential when it comes to evaluating and improving these ideas.

Coming up with creative solutions involves not only having new ideas, but the new ideas must be useful and relevant to the task at hand. Suppose you need a new marketing strategy for your job. Creativity will be the key to coming up with a new strategy. Still, critical thinking will evaluate how good the strategy is looking at how it will affect the company long term and taking into account how your audience might react to it. So, when coming up with something new and innovative, you will find that critical thinking is very useful for selecting the best ideas and modifying them when necessary.

**It Is Important for Self-Reflection**: It is important to justify and reflect on values and decisions in any situation in life. This is critical for living a meaningful life and structuring your life the way you want it to be structured. You may choose to live by a certain religion, a set of core values, or following the teachings or philosophies of a prominent person you admire. No matter what it may be that you choose to structure your life after, critical thinking plays a key role in that.

It is necessary to evaluate what that structure is from an objective standpoint. This is how you avoid passive thinking. Without evaluating your life and what you live by critically, you will find yourself following others blindly without really thinking about what that means. From a critical thinking standpoint, you take control of your own life by evaluating and reflecting on yourself to discover what you should be doing and how you can improve yourself. This process is ongoing, and this is how people evolve positively throughout their lifetime.

**It Is A Domain-General Thinking Skill**: This means that critical thinking can apply to any category of thought. Critical thinking does not limit itself to one subject. Education, research, finance. Technology, management, law, or science; you can apply critical thinking skills no matter what subject you are in. Being able to think well and solve problems is an asset for any career that you choose to go into.

**It Is Useful for Interacting with Society**: Critical

thinking is useful for the benefit of society; it improves how we interact and how we impact the world around us. Some examples of this are science, democracy, and the current knowledge economy. Science may be the main field that people picture when it comes to critical thinking because of its use of experimentation and theory confirmation. The functioning of a democracy depends on people utilizing critical thinking skills because it informs the judgments people make and the things they vote on.

A lot of the world today is driven by information and technology, both things that also require vast critical thinking skills. These things require flexible intellectual skills and the ability to analyze information and solve problems. These are things that are important in a fast-paced and quickly changing workplace.

Critical thinking also informs the interaction people have with those around them. Therefore, it is best not to judge others, draw false conclusions, or be closed-minded about people who are different from us. If everyone utilized critical thinking skills, they would broaden their perspective and be much more welcoming to other people's points of view.

From there, people can work closely together to solve the problems of the world. The more people gathered from various and diverse disciplines, assembling to solve our many problems, the better our society will be prepared for the future. [4]

Critical thinking has seemingly endless benefits in a variety of situations. It is essential for getting the most out of life. When you implement critical thinking, you will find improvements across many aspects of your life, from communication to education to interaction with society.

Now that you know how important critical thinking is, there are a few basic ways that you can implement critical thinking into your life daily. [3]

**Watch**: Observing the world around you is a key first step to critical thinking. Watch what is going on around you, the people you encounter, and how global, local, and personal situations play out around you. Watching is also critical to a few important elements to critical thinking. One of them is broadening your perspective. This is very important to critical thinking because it allows you to see other people's points of view and expand your perspective so that you can form a more objective opinion about the world.

Another key element of critical thinking that you pick up by watching is learning. Expansive knowledge is essential to critical thinking because you have more of a base to work with when developing arguments, conclusions, and opinions. Watching is just one way of acquiring the necessary knowledge on a variety of topics and expands your means of critical thinking.

**Think**: This might seem like the obvious answer when it comes to critical thinking. However, there are a few elements that make this more than simply thinking. As critical thinking is a metacognitive skill, meaning that it is a higher-level cognitive skill that involves thinking about thinking, you must follow the correct rules of reasoning if you want to think at this advanced level.

**Dig Deeper**: This is the main action that sets critical thinkers apart from the rest of the crowd. Most people would come to the first solution that comes to their mind, and that would be the end of it, but the critical thinker takes it a step further. The critical thinker does not settle for any conclusion and instead digs deeper and deeper until they find the answer that is completely satisfying and leaves no room for more questions.

**Discuss**: The critical thinking process does not stop

at your conclusion. One of the characteristics of a good critical thinker is that they are open to other points of view. Once you have come to your conclusion, it could be beneficial to discuss it with others.

Discussing your thought process and conclusion with others can apply to several situations, whether you are finding a solution to a work problem, doing a final presentation for school, or even deciding what to do about redesigning your backyard. By hearing an outside perspective, you can explore other points of view and inform your conclusion.

You might find that there were flaws in your conclusion or something that you had not thought to take into account. This does not mean that your critical thinking was bad. On the contrary, this serves to enhance your critical thinking by bringing in an outside perspective, which can give you ideas that you can incorporate into your next problem.

There are seven thinking habits, measured by the California Critical Thinking Disposition Inventory, which you should try to incorporate into your everyday thought process. Consistent practice of these can immensely improve the way you think.

**Truth-Seeking**: Try to understand the way things are, and if something does not seem right to you, make it a point to find the truth.

**Open-Mindedness**: Be receptive to new ideas, and even if you do not agree, give them a fair hearing.

**Analyzing**: Attempt to understand the reasons behind things.

**Systematicity**: Be systematic in your thinking. This involves breaking down complex problems into simpler parts.

**Confidence in Reasoning**: Be confident in your judgment. Don't always turn to other people for validation and evaluate your thinking.

**Inquisitiveness**: Be curious. Always ask questions, especially if you are not satisfied with an answer.

**Mastery of Judgment**: Don't jump to conclusions and take into account the experiences of others.

The critical thinker does not rely on gut feelings and would rather figure out the answer to a question on their own without being handed the answer. This is what makes this step in the critical thinking process so crucial. Following the process of critical thinking, you would have, at this point, created a question for yourself and gathered all of your information and applied it to conclude. To dig deeper, this will require more research and the elimination of any chance of outlying problems.

Here, you might ask yourself a few questions to guide you:

- What conclusions can I draw, given what I know?
- What can I rule out?
- What does this evidence imply?
- What additional information do I need to resolve this question?
- What are the consequences of doing things that way?
- What are some alternatives I haven't yet explored?
- Are there any undesirable consequences that I can and should foresee? [3]

# Starting To Think Critically

There are a few characteristics that are essential to being a critical thinker. These include broad knowledge, the ability to examine reasoning and the biases around it, the ability to remain calm and collected in the face of uncertainty, and being properly informed about a subject. One of the most important characteristics a critical thinker can have, however, is curiosity.

The cliché saying is that "curiosity killed the cat," but the case of critical thinking is exactly the opposite. You could say that curiosity frees the cat because by being curious and asking questions, you open your mind to new possibilities.

When you ask the right questions, that is how you succeed as a thinker because questions are what powers our thinking in the first place. When you discover something and ask questions about it, your thought process does not stop at just taking what you learned at face value. When you ask questions, you gain more knowledge, and that knowledge allows you to build a better argument, form your own opinions and avoid being a passive thinker.

How often does your mind wander? One moment you could be focused on one thing and the next, find yourself completely out of the left-field with your focus on something entirely unrelated. Asking questions serves to bring clarity to your thinking and set forth a defined agenda for your thinking. Questioning leads us in one direction and determines the information you are seeking. [21]

You can consider critical thinking a journey, and questions are the steps towards your destination.

Here are a few benefits outlining the importance of asking questions when putting critical thinking skills into play: [5]

**It Allows You to Explore Topics and Argue Points of View**: When talking with another person, asking questions allows you to carry the conversation on by creating a meaningful conversation with that person. By asking questions, you learn more about the other person's perspective, which can, in the end, serve to inform your perspective on the subject. You can pursue a topic that appeals to you, defend ideas that are meaningful to yourself, and sharpen your thinking skills.

**It Gives You A Platform to Debate with Others**: Similar to arguing other points of view, asking questions allows you to debate your ideas with others. This is useful because it provides a stimulus for learning as well as a reason for you to learn more about other topics. Also, asking questions keeps the conversation going; otherwise, it would be pretty one-sided.

**It Provides You with Information on Comprehension and Learning**: As you are engaged in a conversation, or even afterward, evaluate yourself in that situation and the critical thinking skills that you utilized. The types of questions you asked and the way you make sense of the answers are great determinants of how well you have comprehended what you just heard. This can help inform you of how well your critical thinking skills are coming along and what you can improve on.

**It Allows You to Find Out What You Think**: As you ask questions, you also discover your opinions and reactions to what you know. Is this something that you can agree with, or are you still skeptical? The more questions you ask, the more you will inform your conclusion on the topic.

When you think of back and forth questions, and answer dialogue, one of the most common scenarios you may picture in the classroom. Most of us have experienced being in a class where the teacher asks questions to create an ongoing dialogue between the students and the students, in turn, ask questions to strengthen their knowledge and learn more from their peers.

Outside of a school environment, you can take those questioning skills and apply them to your critical thinking to further examine various topics through the use of the application, analysis, evaluation, and synthesis as well as gathering and recalling information.

One of the models used in the classroom which you can easily apply to your thought process was one used by Socrates where, through the use of questioning, he encouraged his students to explore prior-held beliefs and, in turn, to build stronger and more scholarly views.

While scholars using the Socratic Method were not

necessarily searching for a right or wrong answer in their students, the main idea was to inspire the students to reflect on their thinking. Respecting an individual's experiences, understandings, and knowledge, Socrates believed that through questioning, previously attained knowledge could be used to develop a thinking which is supported by rationales and logic. [5]

As a critical thinker, self-reflection is imperative to our success in the practice of critical thinking. Critical thinking involves questioning our interpretations in addition to the interpretations of others. Now and then, take time to examine your own beliefs and why you possess them.

Whether you are questioning yourself or the intentions and arguments of others, the answers that you find might inevitably raise new questions, and that is when you know you have reached a milestone in critical thinking.

As you continue to develop your critical thinking skills, don't stop questioning. Question everything until you have all the reasons and arguments in the right place. Questions are even more important to critical thinking as they serve as a tool to skip the rhetorical talk and being manipulated by the media. [19]

When you are first starting with developing your critical thinking skills, you might not be used to constantly asking questions about everything that happens around you. Luckily, there are a few basic questions that you can ask about any situation to start.

Some questions can be used in numerous life situations and can help you make a deductive argument and conclusion. We refer to these questions as the 5 W's and H questions. Not only are they easy to remember, but they leave room for the opportunity to open the door to many other follow-up questions. [9]

## Question Who

This answers the questions of which individuals are involved in the conversation. When asking who, some of the questions that might come to mind are:

- Who benefits from this?
- Who is this harmful to?
- Who makes decisions about this?
- Who is most directly affected?
- Who would be the best person to consult, etc.?

Let's apply this to a real-life example. Suppose one of your most intense passions in life is assisting children, and your vision is to start a nonprofit where you can give children in need educational and enrichment services. When formulating a plan like this, a great place to start is asking questions. Not only will this lay the foundation for what you are doing, but it will also help you to start working out the kinks of what your priorities are within the project. The 5 W's and H questions are a great place to start.

Starting with whom, the obvious answer is young children, but that's when you want to start going a bit deeper. Use the sub-questions as a guiding point and soon begin to develop your questions in the who category. You might explore the specific age group you are trying to target, where they live, where they go to school, and their income level. You would even consider involving other individuals in this project, besides children. This begins the chain of critical thinking.

## Question What

The questions are going to deal with the various functionalities, data, inputs, outputs, deliverables, and artifacts of the topic. Some of the questions you would ask include:

- What are the strengths and weaknesses of this topic?
- What is the other perspective?
- What would be a counter-argument?
- What is the best- and worst-case scenario?

Now apply these to our true to life example. This is an important phase when coming up with any kind of plan or strategy because it's when you start getting into the logistics of it.

When starting these nonprofit things like strengths and weaknesses and best- and worst-case scenarios are important topics to consider because it might end up being the guiding factor in your plan. Best case scenario, you have a flourishing organization that helps hundreds of children. Worst case scenario, it completely falls apart within weeks of getting started. What strategies are you thinking of putting into place to avoid the worst-case scenario? What would the rest of the community think? What would be your overall mission statement?

## Question Where

This explores the geographic location of your topic. While this can seem simple on the surface, there are some in-depth questions you can ask as it relates to this.

- Where are similar situations?
- Where in the world would this be a problem?
- Where can we get more information?
- Where will this take us?

Looking at the nonprofit example, the most basic place to start is where the organization should be located, but then it gets a little more complicated than that. You'll want to look at where most of the children you will be working with are located and plan accordingly for where you will pace your own business. You may also want to consider whether you would have multiple locations or if you want to have a mobile business.

However, the questions asking where can go beyond just geographic location, though. You would want to consider where others who have done similar endeavors located their businesses, where you can get advice, where your employees or volunteers would come from, and where you see your business in the future.

## Question When

This all comes down to the timing of your topic. Similar to the where questions, this can be more in-depth.

- When would this cause a problem?
- When is the best time to take action?
- When will we know we've succeeded?
- When can we expect this to change?

- When should we ask for help with this?

Here you will explore basic questions such as when will you officially open, when will you meet with the children, and when will you host events or classes?

Like the where questions, a little bit of critical thinking comes into play when you start to explore these questions further. You might consider whether the best time to take action is during the school year, where children are immersed in academics or during the summer when they don't have the extra burden of school. When can you expect there to be downtime in the number of people that you have participating and when can you expect the most people? When do you have children graduate from your program, and when do you follow up with them?

When you know you have succeeded is also an essential question to ask. That's when you know you are doing the right thing with your organization, but it will also let you know when you should start striving for more as not to become complacent.

## Question Why

This deals with the various drivers or constraints placed upon your situation. Why is it a critical question to ask when you embark on any plan or project? Anyone can say that they want to do something, but for it to truly be successful, there must be a reason for it. Some questions you can ask when you start asking why are:

- Why is this relevant to them or us?
- Why is this a problem or a challenge?
- Why have we allowed this to happen?
- Why has it been this way for so long?

Whenever you start a new project, initiative, or even a new conversation topic, having a reason for it is essential for the longevity of whatever that may be.

Think of any organization, business, or service you know of, and try to imagine the reason that they came up with it in the first place. Cars? A faster way to get around. Internet? A way to communicate worldwide. There is a reason behind everything.

So, taking our real-world example, why start a nonprofit to provide services for children? Maybe you have noticed disparities among income levels in your community. Or there is a lack of enrichment services within the schools to benefit the children. You also want to explore why things are like this to begin coming up with long-term solutions to remove the problems completely.

## Question How

By asking these questions, this is how you get your project rolling. These questions require you to think deeply about what you are trying to accomplish, but they will be a guiding force to how you begin to implement your plans.

Some of the questions you can ask by asking how are:

- How does this disrupt things?
- How do we know the truth about this?
- How does this benefit us or others?
- How do we see this in the future?

Think of how questions are our real-life example of the real jumping-off point to how you will get into the process of putting your organization into action. First, answering how you want to make changes in your community and how you want to benefit others is a great first step to thinking about what direction you want your plans to go in.

Then ask how you are going to implement your nonprofit, but you will want to be as specific as possible. Instead of simply asking how you will implement the project, but narrow down your questions to how do you want to start, how you want the organization to run, and how you will get people interested. [9]

# Being Successful In Business

Picture the owner of a successful business. They sit in their office pondering the company that they run and the millions of questions that run through their mind daily on running their company in the best way possible and creating the best results for their customers and employees.

One of the situations at the forefront was the empty spaces in the company that needs to be filled with new employees. A stack of resumes and interview notes sit on their desk as the question remains of who would be the best person to hire for the job.

The company started at the beginning of the year and has been very successful six months into it. The goal now is to start expanding by creating more products and getting the company name out to more people. As the business owner, the question on their mind daily is what the best way to do this is? What strategy should the company use? What is standing in the way? What are the strengths and weaknesses of the ideas that the employees have already discussed?

Another thing that comes with that expansion is when the best time to do it is? The business owner, of course, wants to see the company flourish and wants to launch new initiatives at the right moment. Also, the company has laid out long-term goals and milestones, and while everyone works hard to the best of their ability, it can be a long road getting there. When will all of the hard work pay off, and when will they reach their peak of success?

One of those goals is opening a second location. Lately, the business has been doing so well that opening a second location is a plausible consideration. But where would be the best spot to open it in? Where is the perfect place that can reach old and new customers?

Despite all of the successes coming upon the company's first year in business, there have been some setbacks. This does not worry about the business owner too deeply because they understand that every company will deal with some growing pains and bumps along the way. However, they do wonder why these setbacks have happened. Trying to figure out why it will ensure that they do not happen again.

The business owner wonders all the time, the perfect way to get the company booming to be the national and international business that they envisioned. How can they achieve these goals? How can they disrupt the market and make a splash with their products? How can they get to the top of their success?

The 5 W's and H questions can apply to any number of situations and workspaces. In business, employers and employees must ask these questions constantly to keep the business running smoothly but also reaching new heights as often as possible.

Yet, the world is ever-evolving, and the world of business is constantly shifting. In today's world of fast-paced work, technology changes on the dime, and people are constantly in the mindset of immediate gratification. Thus, the 5 W's and H questions are even more critical to the business world.

The better you can master elaborating on those six questions and applying them to your everyday life in the most efficient way possible, you will find that it will have a positive influence on your work. It will help to clear your mind and allow you to run your business endeavors even smoother. This also allows you to reach a sense of clarity within your mind as opposed to disorganized thoughts.

Filtering out extraneous information and focusing on the critical factors of your work in fast-moving industries, is a critical skill coming under the umbrella necessary to be labeled a critical thinker in the business world.

Consider the industry of content creation. In the digital world of today, content creation is hugely important for business because it allows the business to connect with its audience. This can include social media posts that encourage interaction from your audience, blog posts, videos, newsletters, and more. The idea is to create quality content consistently to bring your audience closer to your business community.

The 5 W's and H questions can be instrumental in guiding ideas and create a guideline for content for the business. Following the basics of the six questions and the extended questions that come with it, you might also consider asking, "what if?" as well. Here, you would ask yourself what if everything worked as it should, what if it didn't work out, and what if this topic didn't exist?

With this process of brainstorming, the key is not worrying too much about your ideas being perfect at this stage. Focus on quantity, not quality, and once you have all of these ideas written down, then you can start to filter out which ones are viable options.

In the case of the content creator, they would follow the guidelines of the 5 W's and the H questions, answering each one and writing down as many answers as they can come up with.

So, for Who questions, they might determine that the content creators and the consumers would benefit from the project; it is not harmful to anyone, and the people who make the final decisions would be the supervisors and managers. For when questions, they would brainstorm that the best time to take action would be at the beginning of the writing process and use brainstorming techniques before doing any writing. They will know they have succeeded when the content reaches their audience and people engage with it. And so on with the other questions.

Finally, they can take that opportunity to narrow down their answers into viable options that they can put into action. The final answer to the who question, in this case, would be the company's audience.

- What is the creation of quality content for the audience to consume?
- When is brainstorming ideas before the writing process and putting out the content when finished?
- Where would be the company's website or other selected media platform?
- Why would they engage with their audience?
- How would they engage with their audience by writing and creating engaging content? [9]

There are a few other strategies business people can implement into their daily critical thinking processes besides the 5 W's and H questions. Skills such as analytical thinking, developing interpersonal relationships, and finding a sense of purpose are key elements in the critical thinking process that are often overlooked but are essential towards maximizing your critical thinking skills.

**Being "Successful" Means Finding a Sense of Purpose**: People can have more fulfilling careers if we can focus on the purpose. This is the key to finding motivation and happiness in life. Once you identify your 'Why,' it would be much easier to excel at your 'how.' This process also includes finding out the specifics of what is important instead of assuming that everything is important. This is where the process of narrowing down questions and coming to definitive conclusions in critical thinking comes in.

**Be Wary of Assumptions**: Basing critical decisions on preset assumptions can cause an individual to overlook the important differences a particular group of people brings to the table. A critical thinker's curiosity is one of their most important characteristics. Instead of making assumptions — question everything. If you are not asking these questions and seeking out more, there may be better, more efficient, and better styles that you never thought of before would be missing because you have just accepted the norm instead of finding out more for yourself

**Focus on Resilience**: Another key characteristic of a critical thinker is to remain resilient in the face of adversity. This is an overall important life skill to have because when you find yourself blocked by any kind of obstacle, you can push through it and keep achieving. With a sense of resiliency, you understand that what worked before will not always work the next time. You know that you have to have more options and a broader palette. However, being resilient does not just mean being tough; it means being flexible in light of unforeseen scenarios. You may have something planned out down to the minutest detail, but when something goes wrong and changes the trajectory of your plan, you do not give up. You adapt and find a new way to achieve your goals.

**Be Honest About Your Biases**: There are a few ways to counteract bias. One is getting experience. Experiencing different parts of the world, different points of view, and different types of people is essential for broadening your perspective. The other way is to look for disconfirming evidence — this means actively search for it. If something does not go according to plan, find new ways to succeed in your ventures. If someone has an opposing viewpoint to yours, listen to them, and attempt to understand. You might find out something new that you would never have thought of implementing before. Finally, take a look at your business and social circles and find a way to vary them so that you can discover new points of view.

**Develop a Mitigation Strategy**: Some problems are not as easy to solve as they look to be on the surface. You can find the easy solution and fix it, but in the long run, to solve the real problem, you must find out the core of the issue and solve it from there. Identifying the core problem involves studying the situation and developing a mitigation strategy. In this situation, it is critical to revisit the "Why" category and to ask the question, "Why might this not work?" By starting with this question, it allows people to build mitigation strategies on the front-end and to figure out alternative plans in advance.

**Broaden Your Experience Set**: If you ever find yourself stereotyping, or over-generalizing based on your own experience, it is because your dataset is too narrow. The best solution to this is to go out of your way to spend time with people who are radically different than you. It might be uncomfortable, or even scary, at first. However, getting a sense of what others think and experience serves as a way for you to gain new experiences that you can use to improve your interactions with others. You should view new experiences as new opportunities. Branch out, listen to alternative viewpoints, and keep a fresh outlook.[7]

# Critical Thinking In The Professional World

Business is not the only profession where critical thinking is necessary. Critical thinking is essential to any profession you can think of. Retail? You will have to use critical thinking skills to solve problems daily and try to meet the needs of your customers. Journalism? You use critical thinking to evaluate the newsworthiness of a story and determine whether a story that seems simple on the outside has a deeper impact. Trades? These involve utilizing a unique set of skills to create or fix things and solve problems as they arise.

Everywhere you go, and with anything you do, critical thinking is a skill that is extremely necessary for all aspects of the workforce. It allows employers and employees to look at a situation from all angles and weigh every solution possible before coming up with a direct answer.

There are a few specific ways that critical thinking is beneficial to any profession: [23]

**Coming Up with New Ideas**: Collaboration is a key factor that helps any company to stay afloat. There are few professions where you will not have to work with others at some point to come up with new ideas to benefit the company. Critical thinking brings about new ideas because you go in with an open mind and do not judge or dismiss the ideas of your co-workers before hearing what they have to say. Your ideas join with others to enhance them, and vice versa, and the group looks beyond conventional solutions to efficiently address problems.

**Fostering Teamwork**: When everyone gets involved in the critical thinking process, the workplace becomes more efficient and organized as everyone is thinking to their fullest extent. Especially if the workplace is diverse, everyone brings their own experiences to the table, and someone might bring in something that others would not have thought of before just because they have not had that same experience. Critical thinking promotes workplace tolerance and gives everyone a chance to have an impact on the future of the company.

**Creates Options**: Not only does critical thinking encourage people to work together and come up with new ideas, but it allows people to come up with multiple solutions to one problem. The situation may require more than one solution that an individual may not have thought of otherwise, or it may only require one solution. Still, the company has several options that they can now use to solve the problem. It also allows for the chance to use resources that are already available instead of having to spend money on new things. Additionally, it gives customers options, as well.

**Uncovers Spinoffs**: While the group can come up with options for one solution, critical thinking allows for completely new ideas to come out of those solutions. You and your co-workers may be talking about one thing, and suddenly someone comes up with how to apply that option differently. Once you start asking questions and coming up with ideas, you can address other unsolved topics. [23]

While critical thinking applies to all professions at different levels, there are some professions where critical thinking is imperative to the success of not only the worker and the company. The choices made through critical thinking have a major impact on the people they are involved with. In these professions, if the thinking is not critical and not supported by truth arguments, the consequences of that can be fatal or very dangerous.

## Lawyer

Critical thinking is immensely important in this profession as lawyers have to make decisions in their cases that will have a direct impact on the futures of their clients. This involves using careful judgment and judicious evaluation. Lawyers have to be able to question and analyze what they hear, what they see, what they read, what they feel, and what they think. Lawyers understand not to take first impressions at face value and dive a little deeper with a more thoughtful analysis.

Lawyers can make distinctions that the typical person would not see; they easily detect the ambiguity. In contrast, others see things very clearly; they can look at issues from all sides without actually stating their position, they can manipulate facts to argue any point persuasively and are oftentimes better at analysis than decision making.

A lawyer must be good at deductive reasoning. This means reasoning from general ideas to specific ones. In the case of a lawyer, this requires identifying issues, stating the general legal rules that apply to the issue, and then analyze the facts in light of the rules of law to formulate conclusions to the case. [18]

Lawyers also use reasoning by analogy, which is when similar facts or principles lead to similar conclusions. So, they will often look for analogies in other cases or fields of law to make arguments that are beneficial to their clients. An example that illustrates this is an employer not being liable for the intentional torts of their employees. By analogy to a similar case, an employer should not be liable for the criminal conduct of their employees.

Another thing that lawyers do that is just as important as making analogies is looking for distinctions in the facts or law and argue that adverse cases do not apply to their client's circumstances. [17]

Law is an expansive industry, and there are a lot of different fields of law. However, no matter how different the field of law is, critical thinking skills are equally essential to each of them.

**Civil Rights Law**: This field aims to find a balance between the government and individual liberties. While a small field, many lawyers who practice in other fields take up a secondary practice in civil rights law on a pro bono, or no-charge, basis. These kinds of lawyers often work for nonprofits, public interest law firms, and law firms with diverse practices.

One of the most famous civil rights cases was Brown vs. Board of Education, which determined racial segregation in public schools in the United States was unconstitutional. Lawyers who supported Oliver Brown, the African American parent who led the charge for the lawsuit, would have had to use critical thinking to compile the key points of his case to argue their case against segregation in schools persuasively.

**Corporate Law**: These fields of law focus on helping clients conduct their business affairs in a way that is consistent with the law, as well as efficient. Their responsibilities include preparing initial business articles of incorporation and handling a corporate reorganization under the provisions of federal bankruptcy law. The areas of corporate law include contracts, intellectual property, legislative compliance, and liability matters.

A famous example of corporate law was Dartmouth College vs. Woodward, where his employees deposed the president of Dartmouth College, and the legislature in New Hampshire then attempted to place the ability to appoint trustees to the school in the hands of the governor of the state. However, the school was a private institution. The original charter of the school was created before the state settled the nature of public versus private charters.

In the case of the lawyer who represented the case, critical thinking was necessary to use deductive reasoning to argue for the case of the school is a private entity and the timing of the creation of its charter.

**Criminal Law**: This focuses on the fundamental issues of the law and personal liberties. Criminal lawyers defend the basic rights that are crucial to the preservation of a free and just society. The two main types of criminal lawyers are criminal defense lawyers, and prosecutors and district attorneys. Criminal defense lawyers represent clients accused of a crime while prosecutors and district attorneys represent the interests of the state in prosecuting those accused of a crime.

A high-profile criminal case in the United States, dubbed the Central Park Five, involved five teenage African American boys accused of raping a white woman in Central Park, New York. Although the boys were wrongfully found guilty and jailed for many years for the crime they did not commit, the lawyers representing them would have been responsible for proving their innocence. From a critical thinking standpoint, they would have used critical thinking to see the distinctions that would have pointed out the flaws in the argument that the boys were guilty and may have used analogies to other cases to prove them innocent. [8]

## Doctor

Critical thinking is especially important as a doctor because the lives of their patients are in their hands - literally. The decisions doctors make are the difference between life and death for their patients.

They determine what medicine their patients need to keep their ailments at bay, the best types of treatment for various diseases, and whether or not surgery is necessary to improve their condition. Therefore, critical thinking is essential to a doctor's effective decision making. [13]

Although there are so many innovations in modern medicine that include technology like robots and high-performance computing as well as things like molecular biology and DNA analysis, the power of critical thinking will always be important to the medical practice.

One of the most important steps towards treating a patient is properly diagnosing them with whatever medical failure they have so that the doctor knows how to proceed forward with the treatment process. Cognitive missteps cause many medical errors. According to Jerome Groopman, a fellow of the American College of Physicians (ACP), and Endocrinologist Pamela Hartzband, in an article for the medical publication ACP Internist, medical studies have shown that misdiagnosis occurs in around 15% to 20% of all cases. Further, about 80% of these cases result from cognitive errors.

Critical thinking benefits medical practitioners in

several ways. It helps them to avoid medical and clinical errors and identify better alternate options for diagnosis and treatment. Also, it increases productivity and leads to better clinical decision making. Further, it helps them to work in resource-limited settings, which leads to quality thinking and quality work output. This brings innovation through creativity, helps to avoid litigations, and serves to develop confidence in their practice.

Doctors must be skilled in the art of meta-cognition, or the ability to think about their thinking. This provides them with an understanding of how information can be misinterpreted or misleading, and awareness of this is more likely to reduce their own biases and cognitive pitfalls.

Making a correct diagnosis also involves arranging information from the patient's symptoms, signs, and laboratory findings into a pattern, and applying it to a template of a typical case in the doctor's mind. With the assistance of medical textbooks and evidence-based protocols, clinicians use critical thinking to analyze the symptoms their patient is having and determine the likely diagnosis in typical cases. [10]

However, cases are not always easy to decipher and may contain misleading information. In this case, critical thinking becomes even more important in attempting to determine the exact diagnosis or returning to their analysis if, indeed, they are wrong. This resiliency is a critical thinking characteristic that is necessary for doctors to possess.

A perfect example of critical thinking in the medical field comes from the popular TV show House M.D. This show follows the main character, Dr. Gregory House. His superb critical thinking skills help him to solve medical mysteries in his hospital. The vast majority of the time, his team is unable to come up with on their own because House possesses the ability to look at things from a unique angle and deeply analyze his cases to come up with the correct diagnosis.

Although Dr. House is quite cynical and has a lot of personal demons, there are a few key critical thinking skills that he uses in his diagnosis that are important for any doctor:

**He Takes Risks**: Dr. House is constantly taking risks in his cases. Often, everyone on his team believes one thing is wrong with their patient, but House insists that it is something else. He follows that gut instinct to follow up on his premonition. If he didn't look beyond the surface of the patient's symptoms and go out on a limb against what everyone else says many times, he would not be able to diagnose his patients with the correct illness.

**He Doesn't Always Follow the Rules**: One of the most defining characteristics of Greg House is that he does not follow the rules. Sometimes that gets him into major trouble. But sometimes, it epitomizes a special trait that any doctor could enact in their real life. We should be cautious about breaking the rules, but it is sometimes necessary for critical thinkers to follow their instinct on it.

**He Understands the Importance of Accuracy**: Accuracy is critical in the medical field; a misstep can be the deciding factor in a patient's life. Dr. House would go to great pains to ensure that his diagnosis and administration of treatment to a patient were accurate, and when he was wrong, he immediately went back to the drawing board. He never settled for the obvious answer, such as the other doctors who would insist that numerous ailments were a result of lupus - until the one time it did turn out to be lupus.

**He Knows the Dangers of Over-Analyzing**: We know that analyzing data is an important step in the critical thinking process. Over-analyzing, however, is when things can start to get out of hand. Your mind becomes fatigued, uneasiness starts to settle in, and the critical thinking train starts to fall off the rail. While Dr. House spends a lot of time thinking about his cases, he also knows when to take a leisure break and come back to his cases, skills that can be useful to anyone. [15]

## Judge

Think of how important the job of a judge is. Sitting on the bench looking down at the defendant who could be in the courtroom for an endless set of reasons from reckless driving, drug charges, or even murder, the judge is in charge of deciding their fate. The judge decides whether they go to jail and how long they stay there. The judge is the final determinant of whether the defendant is innocent or not. 1

The judge decides a person's fate, and because of that, critical thinking is essential in making those crucial decisions. They must look at the evidence laid out in front of them and evaluate it, analyze it, ask questions, consult with others, and ultimately come to a conclusion based on what they read and hear. They are in charge of finding the truth based on the evidence. If they did not use critical thinking in these decisions, if they did not go through all of the steps and look at the evidence from all angles using the best of their judgment, the consequences of their decision could be detrimental.

A few skills that the judge will use that require good critical thinking skills are:

**Analytical Skills in Multidisciplinary Teams**: Not only will the judge need to analyze the case individually, but there are also several other people that come into play. The judge must take into consideration everyone involved when they make their decision. They will need to synthesize information from the prosecutors, the jury, and the testimony of the defendant and the plaintiff.

**Research and Analysis**: Individually, the judge will need to analyze the information from all of those sources. They might even do a little of their research looking back on previous cases for comparison or referring to certain established laws as guidance when they make their decision.

**Looking at Problems from A Different Angle**: A judge requires critical thinking skills that use analytics and reasoning, and part of that includes looking at a case in a different way than what may seem conventional. Maybe looking at it one way is not making any sense, and looking at it from another would bring more clarity to the case. This also includes looking at different moral and ethical issues and figuring out the right questions that will lead the judge to the best solution. [14]

In court proceedings, the judge is not the only person

who must use good critical thinking skills. The jury must also use deep critical thinking skills. The jury is made up of a group of people with different ways of thinking, and the judge has to rely on whether they have critical thinking and can make an impartial decision that has a massive impact on someone's life.

Throughout the jury process, the members of the jury will need to use their critical thinking skills to come up with the best solution for the case. As part of the jury process, they will:

**Choose A Foreperson**: The foreperson serves as the spokesperson for the jury who will preside over the deliberations and present the jury's answer to the court. Choosing a foreperson requires critical thinking on the part of the whole jury as they determine who may have the most experience in law and criminal justice, or who has the best leadership skills.

**Use Discretion with What They Can Bring into The Jury Room**: There are often strict rules about what the jury can and cannot bring into the deliberation room. These can include outside reading materials and cell phones. They can receive items for evidence such as medical reports, police reports, and audio recordings, but certain personal items might be limited. Especially if the rules seem vague, it requires a person to size up the situation for themselves and makes the best determination of what they should bring.

**Determine When to Ask the Judge for Help**: The jury is allowed to ask for some assistance with their deliberation, such as asking for a testimony to be re-read, asking questions about the law or instructions on a point not already covered by the judge's instructions. This requires special judgment on the part of the members of the jury. They analyze the situation as best they can, and if there are outstanding questions that none of them can answer, they determine that the best solution is to ask for help.

**Deal with A Deadlock**: Coming to a deadlock is not ideal, of course, but it can happen. Now and then, the best jury might not be able to reach a verdict. The judge can then declare a mistrial or order the jury to go back and try again. Critical thinking comes into play leading up to and determining the deadlock. Jurors go through the process of asking questions, examining evidence, and debating amongst themselves. The critical thinking process is supposed to lead to a conclusion, and if the conclusion is determined to be a deadlock, then that is what it is. However, it might also be the case where there are still outstanding questions that the jury has not explored, so it would be useful to run through the critical thinking process again to be sure.[22]

## Accountant

Critical thinking is essential to most professions, and

accounting is no exception. Accountants work with a lot of spreadsheets and financial statements, so critical thinking is useful in helping the accountant to interpret not only the numbers they see but the story behind them.

Additionally, they need to be able to spot trends and irregularities in the documents they examine. Not only that, but they need to be able to come up with strategies to find solutions to those problems. Critical thinking would help an accountant think differently about finding solutions to the problems they see and come up with working strategies. [28]

Critical thinking is also useful in helping an accountant communicate with their clients effectively. For one thing, they need to be able to work effectively in teams. Still, they also need to be able to communicate well with their clients, too, especially if they are not in the same physical location. Often, they will communicate remotely.

They have to be able to explain the information clearly to their clients verbally and in writing. People come to accountants because they do not understand how to interpret the numbers themselves, so the accountant must be able to explain it in a way that is easy to understand. [24]

These things combined help the accountant to become trustworthy to their clients as well as their co-workers. Accountants deal with sensitive information, and careless mistakes can be detrimental, especially when working with a large company as their client.

To be an accountant requires specific skills, and critical thinking can benefit all of them. Apart from the specialized knowledge of accounting, simply general business knowledge is also important. This is a fundamental aspect of critical thinking because the more you know about a subject, then the better you can make decisions and evaluate information within that topic. With general knowledge, you have enough background information to refer to when someone tells you something that you would otherwise have to do more research on. With a broad spectrum of knowledge, critical thinking becomes easier.

Critical thinking is useful in having the leadership skills required of an accountant as well. Critical thinkers can be leaders because they can think through problems clearly and efficiently. They do not get overwhelmed easily because they can organize their thought processes, they communicate efficiently, and they possess critical thinking skills such as analyzing content, strategizing, and explaining. Leadership skills are important in the accounting field because they must be able to develop new insights, manage projects, and motivate and engage team members.

As an accountant, critical thinking is also imperative

in their customer service actions as well. Accountants work directly with clients to assist with their needs, and this is where things such as communication become very important. In a public accounting firm, it helps to retain customers and bring in new clients. Critical thinking helps to determine when the accountant must listen to the needs of their customers, assess them, and come up with solutions. [12]

## Teacher

Although critical thinking is one of the most important and necessary things for a teacher to teach their students, it is also important for the teacher to be well-equipped with critical thinking skills for themselves.

What ends up happening a lot of time when we talk about teachers is that people tend to focus on how much the students need to learn critical thinking and overlook the fact of how important critical thinking is to the actual teacher. The bottom line is that teachers cannot push students to think more critically if they do not do so themselves.

Think of it this way. Teachers encourage students to push their minds to think differently, seeking cooperative behavior from them to free them and allow them to express their ideas and opinions in a constructive manner.

However, frequently the teacher is expected to follow directions without their autonomy and reasoning that comes from their critical thinking. They spend a lot of extra time outside of the classroom studying teaching techniques and preparing lesson plans, but if they do not free their minds, they are less likely to teach effectively. [27]

The creative instruction and innovation that makes a teacher great come from the teacher's own unique set of critical thinking skills that must be appreciated by not only the teacher but the administrators and school system around them. To fully utilize the art form of teaching, the teacher must be fully engaged in the steps in critical thinking that allow them to do so.

Take, for example, a teacher who is developing a new course having to do with memoirs. No one in the school has ever taught a course like this before. However, the teacher has a strong passion for memoirs and felt that their students would benefit greatly from such a class.

The teacher must then develop the course from scratch. They must determine what they will read during the class, deciding what authors and memoirs would have the most benefit in moving the class along and teach different aspects of memoir as well as things the class can realistically read and discuss within the timeframe of the class.

They have to decide what work the class will do to reinforce the lessons they learn, such as writing essays about the reading and workshopping their memoirs throughout the class and turning in a final memoir by the end of the class.

The teacher has to create rubrics, assessments, and come up with questions they want the students to consider. Some of these questions include, "Does the reading public's fascination with memoir suggest a healthy interest in other people?" or "Does it too often indicate a voyeuristic urge to look through the debris of broken lives?" They might also take feedback and advice from their colleagues. Finally, they must determine the end goal of what exactly they want their students to take away by the end of the class.

This seems like a lot of work, but it is all necessary work. The long and involved process of coming up with a curriculum for a brand-new class involves essential steps of critical thinking: asking a question, gathering information, evaluating the information, coming up with a solution, considering the implications, and getting feedback from others.

Education in the United States lays out a set of common core standards that all teachers must abide by to ensure that students across the country are learning the same thing at the same time as much as is possible. The standards had to do with English/language arts, for example, having to do with analyzing complex texts, weighing evidence, making clear and effective arguments, and to working with others with very different views.

Although there is a standard set of objectives that teachers of all grade levels have to abide by, this does not mean that they cannot make their spin on it to make their classroom more engaging.

Because of this, these standards can only be

successful if the teachers think as critically as the students do. The teacher can follow the common core starts as closely as possible, but if they do not put forth critical thinking to make their class want to think critically as well, such as the case with the memoir teacher, then the students cannot be as successful.

The best way for a teacher to teach critical thinking is if they are proficient critical thinkers themselves. Sometimes the teacher might not like the answer of the student, but they have to agree with the logic if it includes critical thinking. For teachers to teach children to think critically, they must improve their social state of mind. [25]

# Follow These Steps To Make Your Life Easier

The benefits of critical thinking in the corporate world are numerous. Whether you are an employee or the business owner, the decisions you make to ensure the success of the company require a certain level of critical thinking, no matter the industry you are in. In certain professions, critical thinking can be the difference between life and death for the people you are helping or making decisions for.

However, critical thinking can be wildly beneficial in your private life, as well. Consistently practicing critical thinking opens your mind, makes your thought processes stronger, improves how you see yourself and the world, and leads to great academic performance and career progression. It is intentional, and it is a specific mindset that drives people to discover concrete information that they can utilize in a practical sense.

Some of the ways that critical thinking can benefit your personal life are:

**It Allows You Make Better Reasoned Decisions**: Critical thinking helps you to analyze better complex problems with much more ease than you would otherwise. It also helps you to avoid the pitfalls of cognitive biases and fallacies.

**It Helps You Develop Your Problem-Solving Skills**: Once you begin to use the critical thinking process in your everyday life, it will come to you much easier than ever before.

**It Helps You to Become A Persuasive Communicator**: Critical thinking will teach you how to build logical and persuasive arguments. This includes developing premises that make sense and lead to conclusions that are sound, valid, cogent, and strong. It can be an argumentative essay for school, an email, or a direct debate with someone else.

Critical thinking gives you a logical approach to being persuasive.

**It Leads to Better Team Management**: With strong critical thinking skills, you will be able to distinguish between emotion and logic, which is immensely helpful in developing a level-headed mindset that is necessary for leading others. It helps you to identify and solve problems effectively as well as drive performance based on sound reasoning. You don't have to think of this strictly within a work perspective, sometimes you can find yourself in a leadership position among your family and friends that requires critical thinking.

**It Makes You Immune to Bad Rhetoric**: No doubt, you will encounter fallacies such as false dichotomy, poor arguments, and people who utilize actions that serve to stop the productivity of critical thinking such as the intellectually arrogant or people who don't respect reason in the first place. Good critical thinkers can spot fallacies and cognitive biases and know how not to be blindsided by them. [16]

With numerous benefits to your personal life, critical thinking can be appealing, but if you are a novice at the art, it can be hard to know where to start. The best thing to do is to utilize the critical thinking process as often as you can. Whenever you have to make a decision, follow the steps in the process, and see how easy it comes to you over time.

The critical thinking process is essential for solving problems that are complex and do not have an obvious answer or an expected solution. Although there is no correct answer to the problems, using the process of critical thinking, you can come to a solution that is reasonable and valid.

These types of problems are the kind that requires a systematic approach, one that critical thinking is perfect for. Without this systematic approach, it would be more difficult or even impossible to reach a satisfactory conclusion that makes sense. So, to achieve the best results for whatever solution you are trying to find, you must follow the steps in the critical thinking process in order and carry them out thoroughly as all of the steps are necessary to reach a sound conclusion.

**Formulate Your Question**: The first step in the critical thinking process is to formulate your question. This will help you to clarify the problem at hand.

Knowing what you are looking for in solving a problem through critical thinking is an essential first step. A detailed question will guide you as you move forward in the process.

To take a situation as an example, imagine that you have decided you want to live a healthier lifestyle and as part of that you want to join a gym. There are two gyms close to you that you want to choose from, and both come with their pros and cons.

So, the question focuses on which gym you should choose?

One of the most important parts of this step is knowing what you are looking for and explaining it in detail to formulate a detailed question. Layout a list of criteria for you to make your decision. In this case of choosing between two different gyms to join, some of the things you might be looking for are the distance from home, how big it is, the amenities that they offer, and how friendly the people there are.

**Gather Your Information**: The next step in solving a problem through critical thinking is to gather all of your information. Information gathering helps you to weigh out the different options presented to you, moving closer to a decision that hits your goal.

Gather as many details as you can about the situation. These include the pros and cons, practical information, and any questions you have about the situation. Explore any judgments, arguments, opinions, and conclusions that you can find about the issue, whether this is looking online, reading it in a book, or speaking directly with others. Ask yourself what evidence can you find about this that back up or even disprove your experience, beliefs, or opinions on the topic.

Think of this phase as going through analysis and interpretation of the information you have gathered as well.

Also, at this step, you should be able to clarify the problem or situation and ensure that you have a clear understanding of the issue you are trying to find a critical solution for. Ask the five W's and H questions to refine your thoughts on the issue. Some of these might include what is happening, who is involved, what are the stakes in the process, and what is the best way to characterize this?

To be even more thorough, into a deeper analysis of the matter at hand. Start to consider other perspectives, beliefs, assumptions, and opinions apart from your own. Do this with an open mind so that you can consider as many options as possible. You should also analyze all of the facts and any metrics available to corroborate the evidence.

Some of the questions you can ask yourself are:

- What are you claiming?
- Why do you think that?
- What are the arguments (pros and cons)?
- What assumptions must we make to accept that conclusion?
- What is your basis for saying that?
- What are the underlying or hidden issues?

- What would success look like for all of the people involved in the problem?

Be as thorough as possible about gathering information because it will inform your answers in the next step.

**Apply the Information**: This is the stage when all of the information you found on the topic starts to come together. Asking a question and gathering information are considered the "Presentation of the Problem" aspect of solving a problem through critical thinking. When applying the information, this can be considered the "Taking Action" phase of the process.

This is where you consider your reasoning and formulate a conclusion to the situation. Additionally, you will try to evaluate the validity of your argument and solution.

During this phase, you will identify and secure the elements needed to draw a reasonable conclusion. Here, you will compile all of the data, statements, principles, evidence, beliefs, and opinions from the previous phases and begin to brainstorm ideas. At this point, you will identify possible conclusions and determine the viability of the conclusion you come up with.

At this phase, there are going to be critical questions you will want to ask yourself before coming to a definite conclusion on the issue.

Some of these are what conclusions can we draw given what I know, what can I rule out, what does this evidence imply, what additional information do I need to resolve this question, what are the consequences of doing things that way, what are some alternatives I haven't yet explored and are there any undesirable consequences that I can and should foresee?

**Consider the Implications**: In this step, you have come up with a solution to the problem at hand, but it is not enough to just settle on the first conclusion you come up with. Critical thinking in problem-solving goes way beyond that.

Now it is time to consider the long-term effects of your decision. Perhaps right now, it seems right, but what consequences will it have in years to come? This is the type of thing you want to think about before you settle with your decision permanently.

This is all about assessing the credibility of the solution you came up with within the "Apply the Information" phase. Here, you want to review any new evidence and ideas generated since you came up with your solution. Evaluate with fresh eyes the validity of the possible solution and probe for weaknesses in your thinking and logic.

Some of the questions you can ask yourself are how credible is the claim, how strong are the arguments, do we have your facts right, how confident can we be in your conclusion given what you now know, what are the consequences of this solution, what would it look like in a year if you implemented this solution?

A strategy you can take to guide the process of considering the implications is to start by recapping the critical thinking process, possible solutions, and how you arrived at them. Think of any flaws that could have been present in your reasoning. Was there any bias in making the decision? Did you pass over or leave or any important information?

Finally, use the above questions to evaluate the validity of your argument or solution. If you can answer positively to most or all of the questions, then it is safe to say that the implications will not have any significant negative effects on you.

If you cannot answer positively to most of the questions, then it is time to backtrack and reevaluate your critical thinking process. This could mean that you need to gather more information or correct information. Also, returning to the beginning of the process to refine your question could improve results.

**Explore Other Points of View**: After you have considered the implications of your conclusion, the critical work is still not finished as you want to be completely sure that you are making the right choice.

This final phase is a chance for you to take a step out of the situation and look at it as a neutral person. Think of this as a moment to explore other alternatives to what you have come up with and see if you can come up with something better.

Exploring other points of view involves speaking to or reading about others who have a different point of view than you. One of the core aspects of critical thinking is being open-minded and able to explore other perspectives. This is very important for figuring out whether the decision you made is the best one and if there is a better one out there that someone else has come to that might fit you better. You might also determine that you can combine someone else's conclusion with yours to make an even stronger one.

Before coming to your final decision, take the time to narrow down your decision, and ensure that this is truly the best decision that you can come to before settling on your solution completely. Take the time to question, confirm, validate, and connect your reasoning to your results.

Ask yourself if you can be more precise on your choice, how good was your methodology and how well did you follow it; how good is your evidence, and is there anything that you are missing before you commit to the decision.

Following this process of critical thinking carefully, your decisions on complex and ill-defined problems will be more thought-out. Although sometimes it can seem like some problems that we face, critical thinking is unnecessary; it is something we use every day in either complex choices or issues that do not seem as complex such as selecting a gym to join. [29]

# Everyday Life Eased By Critical Thinking

Critical thinking provides immense benefits to those who utilize it daily. It strengthens the mind allowing your thought processes to be more organized and bring clarity to your decisions. By practicing the steps in critical thinking as often as possible, in the long-term, you will find that you have an easier time solving problems and making reasoned decisions. Also, you will have a much easier time communicating with others.

Although critical thinking has benefits to enhancing your mind, in a practical sense, it also has benefits in important life decisions that nearly everyone will find themselves making at some point.

Certain decisions that you make will have a huge long-term impact on your life and will have, and the decision you make can either yield positive or negative effects on your going forward. Whether you are buying a house or choosing a place to go to school, you will find that critical thinking comes into play in making such important decisions. You must thoroughly analyze all of the evidence and consider the implications of all of the possible outcomes of what you are trying to do.

## Buying A House

Critical thinking is especially necessary when buying a house because it is a long-term decision that will have an impact on you for possible years to come. Buying a house is one of the biggest investments that you can make, so you must find a place that you can enjoy and be happy in for years to come. Otherwise, if you end up making the wrong decision, you will find yourself miserable living in that house. Also, you will spend more energy to sell the house and go through the process of buying a new one immediately afterward.

The steps to buying a house can seem complicated at first. There are a lot of things that you need to consider. Critical thinking will be important as you consider the quality and size of the house, the number of rooms, the size of the kitchen depending on the number of members in the family, and more.

As you apply the steps of critical thinking to this decision, there are some questions that you will want to consider as you get started. One of the most important is the location of the house. Do you want to live in a rural, suburban, or urban area? Is there a particular city you are interested in? How far away do you want to live from your friends and family and your job? If you have children, you also want to factor in school. What school system do you want to be a part of, and how far from the school should you live? Do the children attend a dance, music, or any other extra-curricular activities? Also, consider the shops close by, the traffic, and the features in the home.

Now gather and apply the information. One of those factors will be finances. Determine how much the house will cost and how much you are willing to spend per month on a mortgage. Gather your down payment and determine your credit score. A lot of research will be involved in the process as you search for the house at the price you want, as well as a realtor.

Once you have gathered all of the necessary information, you've started working with your realtor, and you have narrowed down a few homes that you might want to settle on, consider the implications. This is an important step in the critical thinking process, especially in a decision as big as this one. Is this a good place for you and your family to settle down in the long-term based on the requirements that you have laid out for yourself? Weigh any pros and cons of the house and determine if there are any deal breakers within the cons. Have you gathered any new information, and down it changes any of the information you have already collected?

Also, consider looking at other points of view. What do other people think of the neighborhood and the city you are considering living in? If enough people have bad reviews, is it something you want to take a risk on? Also, get the opinions of family members. This might be especially important if you are a first-time homebuyer. If you have other family members who have more experience in buying a home, ask them for their advice before you make a final decision.

## Choosing A Car

Transportation is a big deal, in some places more than others. In some cities, such as New York City or London, people can get away with not having a car because of dense development and efficient public transportation. However, in some places, a car is essential. The public transportation system may not be very efficient or might not even be available at all. Many places are not very pedestrian-friendly, with no sidewalks or safe ways to cross the street. Also, walking several miles to get to a store is just not practical in certain cities.

If you are the type of person who will rely on your car to get you everywhere from work to the grocery store and will use the car daily, choosing a good car will be essential to your success. You will use critical thinking skills to find a car that you can afford. One that you will not have to spend a lot of money on gas or maintenance expenses. Also, the car should be comfortable and contain the amenities that you want. Making a bad decision in choosing a car can have very expensive and possibly dangerous outcomes for you in the long run.

Applying the steps in critical thinking, the main thing you will want to ask yourself in the beginning is, what do you want in a car? For most people, the price will be the first thing they look at. Determine if you want to pay for the car in full upfront or do you want to put in a down payment and take on a car note. You will also want to consider if you have any preferences regarding the type of car and the size. Suppose it is just you in the car most of the time, you might want to go for a smaller car. If you have kids, you would consider a larger car. You would also consider whether you want a car that runs on gasoline or diesel fuel. For example, diesel costs less, but in the EU, diesel cars are becoming banned due to pollution. Thus, if the EU finalizes its diesel car ban, then it would be impossible to sell your diesel car in the future.

Now begin to gather and apply all of your information. Like purchasing a house, a lot of research will go into this stage. You could go online to search for different types of cars, or you can even go into the shop to take a look in person. Determine the car dealer you will want to go to, and even if there is a particular salesperson, you want to help you. Start getting your finances worked out, analyzing your credit score, and having the car financed with your bank.

As you go through the process of picking out the car, start considering the implications. Is the price of the car something you can follow up on as you continue to make payments on the car? How does the car feel when you test drive it? Do you foresee any mechanical issues with the car that you will have to spend money to fix later on down the road? These are all questions you want to ask as you consider the implications of the car.

Looking at other points of view is a good idea when choosing a car as well. Reviews can be very useful in this process. Look at reviews of not only the particular model of the car but the dealer where you will be purchasing the car as well. If a significant amount of reviews has had a problem with either, it might be a good idea to reconsider. Also, if it is your first time buying a car or you do not have much experience with buying a car, ask a friend or family member who knows more about cars to help you. This can help ensure that you are not overcharged or ripped off in some way, but use your judgment as well in the process.

## Choosing University

The university that you choose to go to has major implications on the new four years or so of your life. The type of education that you get there determines the trajectory of your career path. The kinds of professors and classes you take will have implications on the knowledge you gain on the subject and, in a lot of cases, whether you continue it in the first place. Not only does it mean a lot for your education, but the university you go to also has a lot to do with your lifestyle. If you are living on campus, it can have an impact on your personal and social life, and if you decide to live off-campus, your commute can have an impact on your lifestyle as well.

Critical thinking is huge when making such a big decision. If you do not use your critical thinking skills in making such a big decision, it can have a very negative impact on your personal life and education. You might find that this is not the best school for the major that you choose and because you are not learning in the way you think you should, you do not get the most out of the money you spend on those classes. Worst case scenario, you might be deterred from pursuing the major further and end up quitting. Additionally, if you do not like the social environment of your school, you could end up feeling lonely and depressed.

Let's say you made the wrong decision on your choice of university. If you decide to transfer to one that better suits you, you will not only have to spend the extra time going through the process of choosing a school again, but you may end up having to spend more time in school than you originally intended. People spend way too much money on going to a university for it not to be a decision that they are comfortable with.

As you are choosing a university to attend, there are a lot of questions that you will want to explore as you move forward with the process. One of the major questions will be your major, whether the university offers it and in what capacity. Also, ask yourself what are the most required professions currently, and can one anticipate will the profession be still attractive in the future after one has graduated and does it comply with your talents and affections. Some other questions to consider are the cost and what kind of financial assistance is available, whether you would prefer a large or small school, whether you want to stay on campus or commute and what the on-campus housing is like if you prefer to stay on campus.

Gather all of the information you can about the school. This includes how much it costs to attend the school per year in addition to either how much it costs to live at the school or what the commute will be like (traffic conditions, campus parking, distance). Fill out your FAFSA and any other information needed to gain financial assistance. Determine the requirements for your major at that school and develop a preliminary plan of what you will need to do over the next four years. Also, you should look at what the school environment is like and what extracurriculars appeal to you.

Critical thinking will also come in handy here when you determine the implications of going to the school. Looking at your lifestyle and finances, you will determine how you will pay for the education and whether you need to make any changes to afford it. In some cases, it will take more than four years to graduate and consider if this is something you are willing to do, or would you prefer a different option where you can finish in four years.

When it comes to choosing a university, hearing feedback from others is always a good idea. Some people have better experiences at the school than others, but if you find that things like the food options, the housing arrangements, or the kind of professors do not resonate with you as much as they have with someone else, you might rethink things.

# Do This To Stop Questioning Yourself

Critical thinkers tend to revise their decision less than other people. They are certain of their decisions because they have analyzed arguments in detail.

For one thing, those that use critical thinking have much stronger reasoning skills. Reasoning determines how good people are at decision making because it involves clear problem solving, and the formation of logically persuasive communication, skills that are equally important in all functional domains. Logical reasoning is a learned skill; it takes years of practice, depending on the person. It is a learned skill based on an already established body of knowledge.

Another reason that critical thinkers do not question themselves as much is that they are aware that their perceptions are biased, so they take the time to reflect on them, analyze their flaws and merits and make decisions outside of perceptions that are not beneficial to the situation at hand.

People naturally have biases that they are not aware of or are not educated about. Because of this, decisions are based on an incorrect judgment about a situation or bad inferences that come from these biases.

Imagine a person who is trying to decide on a university to attend. They may be reluctant to go to a top school if its location is not ideal. A decision influenced by the people around them because this person has never actually been to this town; they are not aware that this is a nice place to live. However, because of their internal bias, they are constantly second-guessing whether they should go to this school and might end up deciding not to go entirely.

Now imagine the person who has strong critical

thinking skills. They, too, developed a negative perception of the top school because of the influence of those around them. However, because they are aware of their bias and have strong reasoning skills, they decide to do a little research of their own before they make their final decision. They consult reviews of the place, ask people who have more experience there, and even go and visit themselves to get firsthand experience. From there, they can confidently decide to attend school without any regrets.

Finally, critical thinkers can separate logical reasoning from emotions and moral judgment. A lot of times, people are more easily swayed by emotions and morals than logical reasoning. These things appeal more to the senses as well as a person's feelings of guilt, and they can give into these things more easily, even if the decision is the wrong one.

Take another real-life example, for instance.

Someone's brother is asking them for money. Recently, they lost their job, and their savings are quickly running dry. However, the brother is a known alcoholic, and as much as they try to deny it, the brother is going to spend the money to buy more alcohol.

This person then goes back and forth in their decision on whether to give their brother money. On the one hand, if they give the brother money, he will continue to drink, come to rely on them more for money in the future, and possibly end up getting hurt or arrested because of the drinking.

However, the situation appeals to the emotions because if they don't give the brother money, he may resort to other, more illegal means to get it, or might get depressed and hurt himself in another way. Do they continue to enable their brother to drink, or do they stop supplying him with money in the hope that he will hit rock bottom and want to get help? Against their better judgment, they may continue to enable the brother to drink in the interest of making their brother feel better.

Critical thinking is a strong force against decisions influenced by emotions or moral judgment. Significant knowledge of rhetorical devices and a perspective on moral reasoning comes a long way in making rational and logical decisions. This is especially true when appealing to emotion or moral judgments.

Whether in a workplace situation or your personal life, critical thinking is essential for any form of decision making. Not only that, but it helps you make much stronger decisions and be surer of yourself.

However, there are a few things that can very easily sabotage critical decision making. These include fallacies such as:

**Hasty Generalization**: This is a conclusion that is not logically justified by sufficient or unbiased evidence.

**Perfectionist Fallacy**: This fallacy assumes that a perfect solution exists and that you should keep searching for it before taking action.

**Line Drawing Fallacy**: This presents the alternatives as either there is a precise line to be drawn, or else there is no line to be drawn, or there is no difference between one end of the line and the other.

**Groupthink and Bandwagon Effects**: This is the act or practice of reasoning or decision-making by a group. Group thinking and bandwagon effects follow uncritical acceptance or conformity to the most prominent points of view.

**Ad Hominem Fallacy**: This is a way to divert attention from a genuine discussion of the topic at hand by instead attacking the character, motive, or another attribute of the person making the argument.

**Base Rate Neglect**: When presented with related base rate information and specific information, the mind will tend to ignore the former and focus on the latter.

Cognitive biases can also sabotage critical decision making. Some of these include:

**Confirmation Bias**: This is the tendency to interpret new evidence as confirmation of one's existing beliefs or theories.

**Survivorship Bias**: This involves people concentrating on the people or things that made it past some selection process and overlooking those that did not, usually because of their lack of visibility.

**Anchoring**: Here, people depend too heavily on an initial piece of information offered when making decisions.

**Availability Bias**: This is a tendency to think that examples of things that easily come to mind are more representative of real-life than is the case.

**Authority Bias**: This is when people attribute greater accuracy to the opinion of an authority figure, and their presence influences their opinion.

**Projection Bias**: People assume that their tastes or preferences will stay the same over time. [16]

People who use critical thinking can identify fallacies and cognitive biases and avoid them to make better and more confident decisions. After making a decision, true critical thinkers rarely revise it because they think far ahead.

They can tell themselves things like:

- "I am now logical and analytical with all the information that comes to me and has opened up all sorts of areas of growth for me."
- "I understand people better and have a much greater insight into the motivations of man."
- "I am much better at problem-solving, and it impacts my life from grocery shopping to cutting through the crap in a Black Friday advertisement."
- "I have increased confidence and authority on many subjects because I can see deeper into them than other people."

# A Guaranteed Way To Improve Your Critical Thinking

There are points that are very important to keep up with if you wish to be a critical thinker. They are:

**Grounding Your Thinking**: This is a technique that helps to keep your mind in the present instead of letting it wander around aimlessly to different topics. They are especially helpful in helping someone to reduce anxiety as well as mental focus from a highly emotional state. There are two different approaches you can take to grounding your thinking: sensory awareness and cognitive awareness. You can utilize sensory awareness by honing in on the five senses: noticing your surroundings, holding something with a significant texture, listening to soothing music, etc. For cognitive awareness, you can reorient yourself to your surroundings by asking yourself a series of questions such as where am I, what is today, what is the date, how old am and what season is it? [11]

**Understand Simple Things Deeply**: This is what critical thinking is all about. To get some practice, there is an easy way to practice it every day. Just take something simple like nature, children playing or people you see while you're out shopping, and try to analyze it a little bit deeper. An easy way to do this is to apply the 5 W's and H questions to it. For example, you notice a few deer roaming around your yard. It seems like a basic thing but asks those six questions to analyze it a little deeper. Who led them there? What are they looking for? When do they come out into the open every day? Where do they like to find food? Why did they come to your yard? How do they determine where they wander?

**Clear the Clutter – Seek the Essential**: An important aspect of critical thinking is being organized and seeking clarity in your thoughts. First, practice this in practical situations such as keeping your house free of clutter or keeping your work desk organized. When you practice such actions daily, it makes it easier to translate that to your mind.

Mentally, practice keeping your mind free of any unnecessary information. For example, when grocery shopping, only focus on the groceries that you need to get, do not clutter your mind with thinking about buying extra things that you don't need.

**See What's There**: Practice awareness in your everyday life by staying focused on your surroundings and making informed observations. Wherever you are, take a moment to notice your surroundings and see what is currently there. Are there any particular people you are interested in? What is the scenery like?

**See What's Missing**: While taking notice of what is a part of your surroundings, also take the time to notice what is not there. Observe if there is something or someone that should be there but is not or things that you were expecting to see.

**Final Thoughts: Deeper Thinking Is Better**: No

matter what it is that you come across in your life, attempt to find a way to see it for more than what it is on the surface. A deeper analysis of a certain object or situation will allow you to practice critical thinking. This prepares you for real critical thinking situations.

**Igniting Insights Through Mistakes**: One of life's greatest lessons is making mistakes. So, when you make a mistake, don't give up, don't feel down on yourself or scold yourself for it. Instead, take the time to step back from it and examine it. Determine what the situation was and what exactly went wrong. Ask yourself how you could have done better in that situation and come up with some ideas about what you can do the next time you are in a similar situation to ensure that you do not make the same mistake again. Finally, determine what you have learned from the mistake that you can take into many different situations.

**Welcome Accidental Missteps – Let Errors Be**

**Your Guide**: Embrace the mistakes that come into your life. Accept that not everything is going to go perfectly and that accidents and missteps happen to everyone. No one is immune. Also, understand that those things make you stronger. Apply the lessons that you learn from them to the next situation you encounter, whether it is similar or not.

**Finding the Right Question to the Wrong Answer**: Suppose you are trying to find a solution, and you come to one that does not exactly work. It's time to go back to the drawing board, but what should you change about your process to lead to the right answer this time? A good first step is coming up with a different question. Finding the right question is important because once you find the right question, the right answer will come more naturally to you. It brings clarity and focuses on the issue while lighting up the path to the right solution.

**Failing by Intent**: Being intentional about your

decisions means you are active in your decision making. So, if there is something you are planning on doing, but it ends up not working out, it is more beneficial to have been intentional in the actions leading up to it.

**Final Thoughts: A Modified Mind-Set**: There are times where you make a goal to do something, such as waking up early in the morning to exercise, but by the time the alarm goes off, the motivation to get up and exercise disappears. Instead of simply saying you don't feel like it, make sure you have good specific reasons for modifying your mindset. In this case, you could say you were interrupted and did not get as much sleep as you intended, or your mood changed, but make sure you have good reasons for changing your mind.

**Creating Questions Out of Thin Air**: Sometimes, it is necessary to ask questions, but the exact question you want to ask does not come very easily to you.

When trying to come up with a question out of thin air, you want to think from general to specific. Think of the key points of the situation. For example, your grades are low, and you need to figure out a way to learn more effectively so you can get them up to at least a B to pass the class. Now that you know the general situation, determine the most important factors in that scenario. Here it would be, "How can I study more effectively to pass this class?"

**How Answers Can Lead to Questions**: Answers can be the stimulus for more questions to be asked. Have you ever been in a classroom situation where a student asks one question, and after the teacher answers, more hands shoot up one by one to ask more questions based on that one answer, and the conversation continues in that way? This is because when asking one question, the answer can lead to something you had never thought of before or something else that you want to know.

**Creating Questions Enlivens Your Curiosity**: Think of a small child that keeps asking questions. They want to know why the sky is blue, and once you give them an answer, they ask why and they continue to ask why until you run out of answers for them and have to change the subject. Children are naturally curious and have no insecurities when it comes to the number of questions they ask. Adults can be just as curious. Especially when one question raises even more of them, and you just have to know the answer until you are fully satisfied. When you desire to know something, imagine being the innocent child who wants to know why and come up with more questions until you reach the satisfying answer.

**What's the Real Question?** Although you can come up with questions out of thin air and ask more than one question, the end goal should be to get to the real question. This is the true focal point of your curiosity, the central point that will lead to your conclusion. Getting there might involve asking many questions until you get down to the right one, but the main initiative should be to answer the real question before you form a conclusion.

**Final Thoughts: The Art of Creating Questions and Active Listening**: Creating multiple questions is fine, but just as important is listening to the answers to those questions. This not only prevents you from asking unnecessary questions, but when you fully listen to the answers, you gather more data to inform your next question and ultimately come to your conclusion.

**Seeing the Flow of Ideas**: The formation of ideas and acting on them is what ultimately leads to a sound conclusion. Often, the first idea is not going to be the solution that you settle on. One idea builds off of another until you finally reach a satisfying idea that you have analyzed thoroughly. This process of thinking things through helps you visualize how to proceed in the situation practically. Imagine a work situation where the group is coming up with ideas to grow the company. One employee gives their idea, and the next employee comes up with a way to make it better. A few more people might share their input until the group realizes that this might not be entirely viable in the end, but the next idea uses certain pieces of the last one, and the group builds on that instead. The result is a mixture of all of the ideas that were suggested and discussed.

**Understanding Current Ideas Through the Flow of Ideas**: The flow of ideas also helps you to understand more about the current idea. Suppose at this same business, one idea is already being put into practice to grow the company, but the employer feels like it could be better. Through the flow of ideas, the group discusses what to do; they realize ways that the current idea is not working and how they can improve it.

**Creating New Ideas from Old Ones**: Although an old idea may not be carrying out goals in an ideal way, they provide a basis for new ideas to be formed. The idea as a whole may not be working, but there could be certain aspects of it that are still very good, and you can build off of those to form an entirely new idea.

**Final Thoughts: "Under Construction" Is the Norm**: Sometimes, there is not just one final solution, or the final solution takes a long time to get to. Different ideas are pitched and put into practice that builds off the last idea, and while they may show some progress, they do not get you to where you want to go, and you have to modify it.

**Engaging Change**: Change is imminent. It's not something you can fight; it comes no matter what. It is how you handle change that makes a difference in the outcome. The critical thinker embraces change. They are open-minded and do not let change deter them from making progress. In the process of change, they accept mistakes, ask questions, and come up with new ideas in an attempt to make the best of it and come up with something better.

# The Best Way To Get Started

Like anything, you cannot realistically expect to be amazing at critical thinking the first time you try it. If you are, then that's amazing, but for most people, that won't be the case, and there is nothing wrong with that. For the hew critical thinker, the best way to get better is to practice. The phrase "practice makes perfect" heavily applies to critical thinking.

Your development as a critical thinker will likely be a gradual process, and you will find that you go through phases as you progress. Before getting started, consider yourself the unreflective thinker where you are unaware of the immense benefits of critical thinking. When you just start practicing, you will become a challenged thinker where you have recognized the problems in your thinking and have taken on the challenge of becoming a critical thinker.

From there, you will be a beginner in critical thinking

where you have minimal critical thinking skills. Then, you become a practiced critical thinker where you are getting regular practice. Finally, you will be the advanced critical thinker where you have become advanced in your skills.

Once you become good at it, the final stage in the development of critical thinking is the master thinker. At this point, the skills and insight that come with critical thinking become second nature to you.

If you are reading this book, likely, you are in the challenged thinker phase, where you recognize the flaws in how you have been thinking and understand the benefits to your life that will come with improving your thinking.

As you begin your critical thinking journey, there are a few exercises you can put into practice every day so you can cultivate your skills and start moving towards being a master thinker.

**Use "Wasted" Time**: People often fail to use all of their time productively. Naturally, they want a moment just to take a break, let their minds wander, and decompress from a long day. While taking a break is often very necessary, sometimes this can turn into wasted time, which is, obviously, a negative thing. You jump from one diversion to another without actually enjoying it, you become upset about things you cannot control, or you worry unproductively.

Instead of letting wasted time turn into a negative consequence, use it productively by taking the chance to practice critical thinking. So instead of wasting your time browsing through Netflix without actually finding anything worthwhile to watch or spending time aimlessly scrolling through social media, use it to do some self-reflection. Think over your day and some of your strengths and weaknesses.

There are a few questions you can ask yourself such as when did I do my worst thinking today, when did I do my best, what did I think about today, did I figure anything out, did I allow any negative thinking to frustrate me unnecessarily if I had to repeat today what would I do differently and why? Take it a step further by recording your answers. This way, you can dig deep and reflect.

**A Problem A Day**: Make it a goal to solve one problem each day. At the beginning of the day, choose a problem to work on when you have free moments throughout the day. Figure out the logic and identify its elements. Some of the questions you can ask yourself in that process are what is the problem, and how can I put it into the form of a question, and how does it relate to my goals, purposes, and needs?

Follow this process when solving the problem:

- Take your problems one by one statement is as clearly and precisely as possible.

- Study the problem to make clear the "kind" of problem you are dealing with. This involves figuring out the kind of things you will have to do to solve it and distinguishing them over something you can control versus something you cannot.

- Determine the information you need and actively seek it.

- Collect information and analyze and interpret it carefully. Draw any reasonable inferences.

- Figure out your options for taking action. Make plans for what you can do in the short term and long term and recognize your limitations as far as money, time, and power go.

- Evaluate your options. Take into account the advantages and disadvantages of those options in the situation you are in.

- Develop a strategic approach to the problem and follow through on it. This can include direct action or a carefully thought-through wait-and-see strategy.

- When you do act on your plan, monitor the implications of your actions as they begin to emerge. Be ready to revise your strategy at a moments' notice if the situation requires it and be ready to shift your strategy, analysis, or statement of the problem as more information becomes available.

**Internalize Intellectual Standards**: Each week, make a goal of developing one of the universal intellectual standards. These are clarity, precision, accuracy, relevance, depth, breadth, logicalness, and significance. There are a few actions you can take for each standard:

- State what you are saying explicitly and precisely
- Elaborate on your meaning in other words
- Give examples from experiences you have had
- Use analogies, metaphors, pictures, or diagrams to demonstrate what you mean.

**Keep an Intellectual Journal**: Journaling is a great way to keep track of your progress and reflect on the actions you have taken. Every week, you should write a certain number of journal entries using this format:

- Describe a situation that still is or used to be emotionally significant to you.
- Describe your response to that situation.
- Analyze what exactly was going on in that situation.
- Assess the implications of the analysis and write out what you learned about yourself and what you would do differently next time.

**Reshape Your Character**: Choose an intellectual trait such as intellectual perseverance, autonomy, empathy, courage, or humility, to strive to change each month. While you are working on that trait, focus on how you can develop it within yourself. For example, if you choose courage, you can start by determining what situations or things make you afraid or anxious and then practice slowly exposing yourself to those things.

**Deal with Your Ego**: Everyone has some level of an ego; some people's ego is greater than others. Keeping your ego in check is imperative to critical thinking. Put this into practice by observing your egocentric actions or thinking by asking yourself that following questions: under what circumstances do I think with a bias in favor of myself, did I ever become irritable over small things, did I do or say anything "irrational" to get my way, did I try to impose my will upon others and did I ever fail to speak my mind when I felt strongly about something, and then later feel resentment?

After that, think of ways to replace that thinking with more rational thought and systematic self-reflection. Here, ask yourself: what would a rational person feel in this or that situation, what would a rational person do and how does that compare with what I want to do?

**Redefine the Way You See Things**: Every

situation has a meaning, and everyone sees situations differently based on their perspective and personal experience. How people define a situation determines how we feel about it, how we act on it, and what it means for us. In that case, if you aim to see things in a more positive light, you will respond to them more positively and proactively.

The first thing you can do in this case is to create guidelines for yourself. Create a list of five to 10 recurring negative contexts that make you feel frustrated, angry, unhappy, or worried. Then identify what it is about each case that is at the root of the negative emotion that you feel. Finally, choose an alternative definition for each context and then plan for new responses and new emotions.

**Get in Touch with Your Emotions**: Whenever you feel a negative emotion, take the chance to pull back and ask yourself a few questions to redirect it into something positive. Ask yourself what the thinking is leading to this emotion and how you can change it. So, for example, if you are angry, you can ask yourself those questions and determine that a co-worker is rude. However, you can turn it around and think that they might be going through something personal, and you should try not to let it get to you and instead be kind to them.

**Analyze Group Influences on Your Life**: Most of the time, the people you hang out with have some influence on your life, whether they influence your specific actions or your outlook on life. In the groups that you are part of, closely analyze the behavior that is encouraged and discouraged. Analyze factors such as what you are required to believe in these groups and what you are forbidden to do. Determine what pressure you are succumbing to and whether it is worthwhile to continue.[20]

# Conclusion

Critical thinking is vital in today's world. It does not matter what profession you go into or what life situation you find yourself in, critical thinking plays an important role in each of them. The stronger your critical thinking skills are, the better equipped you will be to make the best decisions for yourself.

Some professions, such as doctors and lawyers, especially require critical thinking because their decisions have major implications for the lives of the people they are working with or representing. When running a business, critical thinking is also imperative to the decisions made that keep the company running long term.

Not only is critical thinking important to your success in the workforce, but it is also the key to unlocking your potential in your personal life. From making major life decisions to minor daily decisions, and not questioning yourself in between, critical thinking ensures focus. When you organize your mind, you can decipher and examine every situation you encounter adequately.

Critical thinkers add value to reasoning by creating universal questions. Applying the 5W's and H questions to nearly anything, the critical thinker can analyze and find clarity in any decision and situation. By opening the mind and moving away from passive thinking, people who regularly utilize critical thinking can have a massive impact on not only themselves but on society as a whole.

Like anything, critical thinking skills do not appear overnight. To go from the unreflective thinker to the master thinker takes time and practice. By following the steps in the critical thinking process every day and using daily strategies to strengthen your critical thinking skills, you will find that, with time, you can unleash a new level of thinking.

# Do you want to...

⇒ Stay up to date and hear first about new releases?

⇒ Get huge discounts and freebies?

⇒ Improve your thinking and have more success in life?

**Sign up for our newsletter and get our thinking cheat sheet as a free bonus! Inside you'll find:** 21 timeless thinking principles you need to know to upgrade your thinking and make smarter decisions (not knowing these may hinder you from having the success you'd like to have in life)

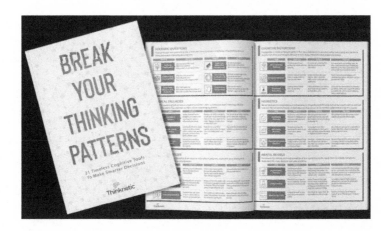

# CLICK HERE TO DOWNLOAD FOR FREE!

Or go to www.thinknetic.net or simply scan the code with your camera

# References

[1]     Baer, Andrew. "How Critical Thinking Relates to Criminal Justice." (2018). *Career Trend.*

[2]     Batmanabane, Gitanjali. Kar, SitanshuSekar. Menon, Vikas. Zayapragassarazan, Zayabalaradjane. "Understanding Critical Thinking to Create Better Doctors." (2016). *Journal of Advances in Medical Education and Research.*

[3]     "Benefits of Critical Thinking." (2019). *Critical Thinking Academy.*

[4]     Chan, Jonathan. Lau, Joe. "What Is Critical Thinking?" (2004). *Critical Thinking Web.*

[5]     Christenbury, Leila. Kelly, Patricia P. (1983). *Questioning: A Path To Critical Thinking.*

[6]     "Critical Thinking: Basic Questions & Answers." *The Foundation For Critical Thinking.*

[7]     De Sena, Joe. "Six Lessons in Critical Thinking from a Professional Critical Thinker." (2015). *HuffPost.*

[8]     "Fields of Law." *Law School Admission Council.*

[9]     Foley, Joe. "A Simple, Sure-fire Way to Create Great Content – The 5 W's & the H." (2011). *WPMUDEV.*

[10]    Groopman, Jerome. Hartzband, Pamela. "Mindful Medicine: Critical thinking leads to right diagnosis." (2008). *ACP Internist.*

[11]  "Grounding Techniques." *Peirsac.*

[12]  Half, Robert. "Accounting Skills You Need to Succeed On the Job." (2018). *Robert Half.*

[13]  Hall, Harriet. "Critical Thinking in Medicine." (2019). *Science-Based Medicine.*

[14]  "Importance of Analytical Skills in Criminal Justice." (2016). *Lamar University.*

[15]  Kaufman, James C. "Channeling Dr. House as I teach Critical Thinking." (2009). *Psychology Today.*

[16]  "Learning Critical thinking is not optional, but essential for good decision making." (2019). *Critical Thinking Academy.*

[17]  Lee, Courtney. *Legal Skills For Law School & Legal Practice.*

[18]  McKeown, Kevin. "Thinking Like A Lawyer Is A Technique - Not A Lifestyle." (2014). *Above The Law.*

[19]  Nappi, Judith S. "The Importance of Questioning in Developing Critical Thinking Skills." *The Delta Kappa Gamma Bulletin: International Journal for Professional Educators.*

[20]  Paul, R. Elder, L. "Critical Thinking in Everyday Life: 9 Strategies." (2001). *The Foundation For Critical Thinking.*

[21]  Paul, R. Elder, L. "The Critical Mind is A Questioning Mind." (1996). *The Foundation For Critical Thinking.*

[22]  Portman, Janet. "Deliberations in the Jury Room." *Lawyers.*

[23]  Root, George N. "What Are the Benefits of Critical Thinking in the Workplace?" *Chron.*

[24]  Rosavich, Anne. "How to spot a job applicant with critical thinking skills." *Accounting Jobs Today.*

[25]  Ruenzel, David. "Embracing Teachers as Critical Thinkers." (2014). *Education Week.*

[26]  "Three Compelling Reasons to Learn Critical Thinking." (2019). *Critical Thinking Academy.*

[27]  Ward, Robert. "Valuing Critical Thinking in Teachers." (2018). *Advancement Courses.*

[28]  Wiley, Sandra. "5 strategies to grow critical thinking skills." (2015). *Journal Of Accountancy.*

[29]  "A Systematic Process For Critical Thinking." *University of Florida.*

# Disclaimer

The information contained in this book and its components, is meant to serve as a comprehensive collection of strategies that the author of this book has done research about. Summaries, strategies, tips, and tricks are only recommendations by the author, and reading this book will not guarantee that one's results will exactly mirror the author's results.

The author of this book has made all reasonable efforts to provide current and accurate information for the readers of this book. The author and its associates will not be held liable for any unintentional errors or omissions that may be found.

The material in the book may include information by third-parties. Third-party materials comprise of opinions expressed by their owners. As such, the author of this book does not assume responsibility or liability for any third-party material or opinions.

The publication of third-party material does not constitute the author's guarantee of any information, products, services, or opinions contained within third-party material. Use of third-party material does not guarantee that your results will mirror our results. Publication of such third-party material is simply a recommendation and expression of the author's own opinion of that material.

Whether because of the progression of the Internet, or the unforeseen changes in company policy and editorial submission guidelines, what is stated as fact at the time of this writing may become outdated or inapplicable later.

whatsoever without the written expressed and signed permission from the author.